a life in the year of...

POETRY AT HIGHFIELD

by Cheryl Moskowitz and the children of Highfield Primary School, North London

Circle Time Press

Published by
CIRCLE TIME PRESS

info@circletimepress.co.uk

First published in Great Britain 2015

Set in Adobe Garamond Pro/Corbel/Moon Flower

Design by Alastair Gavin

ISBN: 978-0-9564082-2-8

Printed and bound by CPI Group (UK) Ltd, Croydon, CR0 4YY

This book charts a poetic journey
through the life of the 2014-15 academic year
at Highfield Primary School.

CONTENTS

FOREWORD
by the Head Teacher, Highfield Primary School

Welcome to *a life in the year of... Poetry at Highfield*. As you turn the pages of this inspiring anthology we hope you will enjoy being immersed in the experiences, emotions, laughter, sadness and joy that these poems evoke.

Working collaboratively with Cheryl Moskowitz the children of Highfield Primary School have found their poetic voices to talk about their lives, learning, dreams, aspirations and families. Poems have been written across all subjects, by all staff and all children, and the ripple effect has reached out into the community and beyond. I am sure you will agree that the poems are truly outstanding and reflect our school's culture, one in which every child strives to excel and reach for the stars!

Maria Kemal

Poetry
at Highfield

introduction

As this academic year nears its end, along with our first Poet's residency, we pause to think back to when it all began on a summer's day in 2014 on a staff training day. Introducing the new English curriculum and specifically the renewed focus on Poetry, the idea of finding a Poet in Residence was voiced. Through word of mouth, we found Cheryl, the journey began and the idea became a reality!

We could not have imagined the impact of having a poet in residence at Highfield. Poetry has touched every curriculum area and has enhanced our children's spoken and written language. The children have embraced and developed a love of poetry that will stay with them for the rest of their lives.

Helen McGovern, Deputy Head Teacher

FIRST DAY AT HIGHFIELD

Close your eyes...
Imagine a school, a little like this one;
big schooly walls
long schooly halls
high schooly ceilings
shiny schooly floors

Pack up your bag...
and imagine the journey;
your go-to-school walk
your what-will-it-be-like talk
your I'm-a-bit-nervous butterflies
as you go through the doors.

Then open your eyes
and look all around;
all the new schooly faces,
the friends you have found
the ones you remember,
and those you forgot
all the things that are different
(there WILL be a lot!)

Then make space in your head
make sure it's quite clear
for everything new
you'll be learning this year

And who knows, just maybe
before you go home
You'll have written your very own
First-Day-at-School poem!

Cheryl Moskowitz

new term

At the beginning of a new school year we are all new and wondering what this year is going to be like. We ask ourselves questions about what we are expecting and what is expected of us. I sat in with a Year 3 class when they were considering their rights and responsibilities, and Highfield's Children's Charter, and these are some of the kinds of things I heard.

It's my right to speak and be listened to.

It's my responsibility to listen to others when they are speaking.

Children have a right to a clean environment at home, at school or wherever they are.

It's our responsibility not to leave rubbish in the classroom, or on the playground.

Children have a right to be educated. A right to go to school.

It's our responsibility to respect others. To believe in ourselves. To be proud.

Class discussions in 'Be Proud Week' led Year 5 to talk about...

PROUD MOMENTS

I got a cat!
I rode the waves in the sea air on the glorious sea,
I did a 360 degree turn in the air on my surfboard,
I went ice skating,
running, hunting… my inner lion!
I was outside chasing antelope on grassland on a sunny day in hot Africa,
I was swimming away from the beach - a big beach full of sand – surfing waves and lots of shells,
Lots of heads looking at me!!
I scored 9 goals in football, I was cheering, kicking the ball in the air… happiness.
I fed six dogs and a rabbit in a cage, trained it to eat cheese.
Once, in a tall building near lots of shops, there was a happy sound,
the noise of people talking. There were people around but it was really quiet,
then suddenly, a baby screaming… 'Her name is Jasmin', Mum said.
I felt really happy. I was really proud.
Like riding waves on a surfboard in the sand or once, at school, when teachers
were talking and there were people in my way and people sat in the hall
and my name was said into the microphone…
Voices cheering!!

school council

One of the most special and important roles at Highfield Primary School is being on the School Council. Members of the School Council have the responsibility to represent their school and their classmates by upholding school values and ensuring that the pupil voice is heard. The School Council has the opportunity to share their views and opinions in a way that can move the school forward and make it better for everyone.

Not everyone gets to be a School Council member. First you have to decide if you want to do it, then you have to apply, be nominated and finally you will be interviewed.

One girl from Year 6, Christina, wrote a poem as her letter of application.

WHY I WILL BE A GOOD SCHOOL COUNCIL CHAIR

I will be a good SC chair
because I'm always very fair
Though I can be harsh at times
I would never commit a crime
I love doing speeches and things
Though I am nothing like a king
Achieving Chair position is my goal
Because I can't wait to take on a role -
Become a model for children to look up to
working to agree new rules and values
When I am older I won't lie in bed, shrivelled
I will get up, stand up, and change the world.

by Christina

When the School Council was elected they had to choose who would play the key roles amongst them. They needed someone to be Secretary, someone to be Treasurer and someone to be Chair.

The topic for the whole school during the Autumn term 2014 at Highfield was Pictures, Portraits and Photographs. It seemed a good idea for the newly elected School Council to present a picture of themselves to the rest of the school.

THE BEAST THAT IS SCHOOL COUNCIL

Respect
Big Friendly face
Here to help our classmates
Making school magic possible
Believe!

our school

At Highfield there are lots of children who are new. Not just new to the school or new to their class but new to the country. Not only do they have to get used to living in a new place - meet new teachers and make new friends -when they come to Highfield but often they have to learn a whole new language as well.

The first things we learn in any language are the names given to things, people and places.

Here is a poem Year 5 wrote about our school, which is called Highfield.

THE HIGHFIELD POEM

Highfield
Half new, half old
Helping kids achieve more
Place of safety and belonging
Sharing

...and this is a poem is by a girl called Şazen who had newly arrived from Turkey and wrote this poem about herself and her name on her first day at school.

Şazen
tall girl smiling
she likes to play football
happy excited…and angry
Magic!

overheard in reception

Poetry is a good way of learning about people
and the things that are important to them.

Here are some poems I wrote inspired by
conversations I overheard in Reception Class
in the first few weeks of school.

STANDING PROUD

Wow, you're a good builder!
Says the girl from Year 1
to the boy in Reception who is just a bit smaller
Well yes I am says the new boy
Building is fun
I'm making this one very, very much taller!

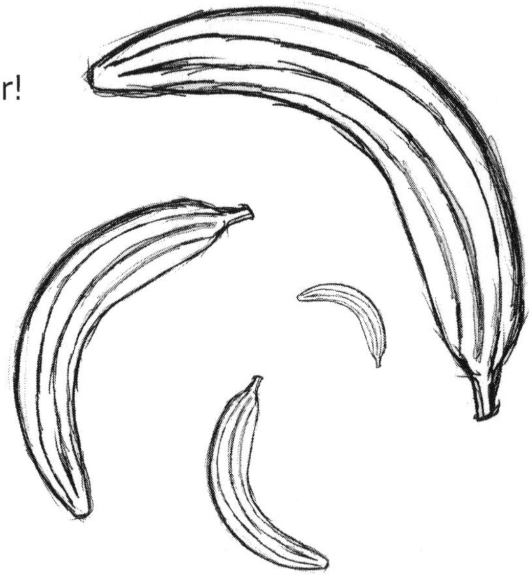

AT THE CORNER CAFÉ

it's closing time
it's opening time
I order toast
I order tea
I ask for bananas, beans and peas
We're out of bananas the café man says

PUDDING

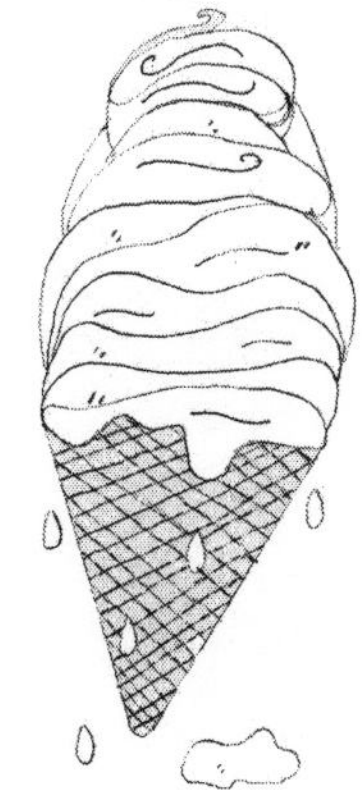

Do you like apple crumble?
I do, at my Nana's –
She makes it with ice cream
chocolate sauce and bananas.
That's not apple crumble
that's a banana split!
Whatever it's called
that's how Nana makes it!

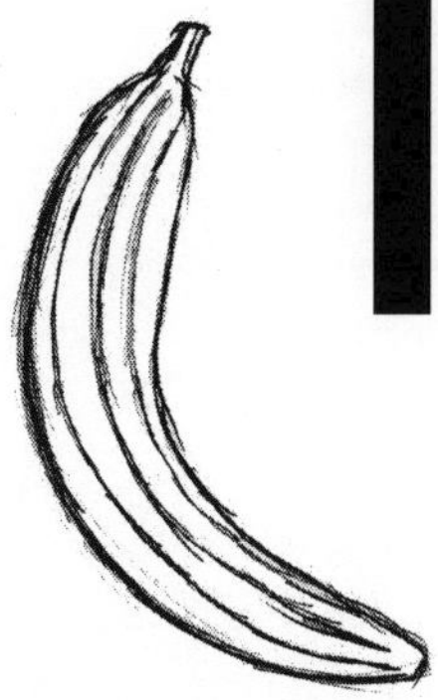

TUMBLING RUMMY

I don't want peas in my tea
I don't want cheese in my coffee
I'd like a Beg and Acon sandwich
and some sticky icky toffee!

Cheryl Moskowitz

my favourite toys

Poetry is a good way of learning about people and the things that are important to them.

Here are some poems children in Year 5 wrote about their favourite toys from when they were younger.

Mikey
Brown like chocolate
Cuddles with my soft toy
Like warming sunshine in my heart
Mikey

by Kushi

Brown dog
Cute eyes, chewed nose
Guarded me, safe and warm
Much loved, came everywhere with me
Darling

by Emileo

Bunny
Fluffy and cute
Bought in Albania
NOT just a toy but my friend too
Special

by Fiona

Builder
Small and yellow
Carrying big objects
Helps me build all my happiness
My friend

by Suber

Lapin
Pink and cuddly
Comfort gift from uncle
Buried deep and loved all the time
Treasured

by Sarah

Blond bear
Fluffy, dusty
It always kept me safe
My fluffy dusty yellow bear
Loved it

by Oliver

Macka
Cute and cuddly
light brown, small and furry
Loved and cherished deep in my soul
Lovely

by Ellie

Toby
Brown eyes, chewed head
Treasured and full of love
Safe in my heart always
Toby

by Zarah

Handcuffs
Tiny and grey
Worn out grip, old favourite
from Dad, carried with me always
locked tight

by Annesther

White Bear
Black eyes, big nose
Keeping me safe at night
Safe and remembered in my heart
Teddy

by Onnoy

Giraffe
Cuddly and soft
Received from my Nan
It will stay in my memories
Best friend

by Emilia

Barbie
has a pink dress
She is made in China
I had her from when I was 1
My doll

by Sutaria

remember

Writing poetry helps us to remember, and a poem is a good place to keep memories safe so you can share them with others when you want to.

The theme for National Poetry Day 2014 was REMEMBER.

Children in Year 2 remembered special moments in special places.

IN OUR WORLD

We can remember…
colourful leaves in the park
being at the beach
at the funfair on a roller coaster with my dad
on a roller coaster with my sister,
a roller coaster shaped like a boat, scary and dark.

We can remember…
a yellow submarine in Legoland
crashing into a Lego car
eating hot dogs in the hot sun

We can remember….
colourful slides
a twirly slide going *bump!* at the bottom
the yellow one was really scary.

We can remember…
being in another country
eating a kind of pasta, with banana
Palm trees with bananas on and animals all around
grey cats and the sound of dogs eating *chomp! chomp! chomp!*

We can remember…
eating *sadza* in Zimbabwe
peanut butter and chocolate ice-cream in Canada
rice with tomato sauce, *dim sum* with Grandma and Grandpa in China
at home eating chips, just plain chips.

We can remember…
being on holiday
Swimming in pools with blue water and the water park in Cyprus
being by the beach and seeing sharks!
And once, getting lost in the Sports shop,
when Mum found me by the clothes.

But best of all places and things to remember…
is being at home in bed

Year 2 children remembered all the things they used to have and don't have any more. They wondered....

WHERE DO THE LOST THINGS GO?

Where do the lost things go
do you know?
Oh where do the lost things go?

My tooth and my teddy,
I looked and can't find them
My fish and my rabbit
I just didn't mind them
My build a bear teddy
with brown and black hair
My best glittery shoes
They're all lost somewhere

Where do the lost things go
do you know?
Oh where do the lost things go?

I'm missing my Aunty
playing games on her iPad
I miss my home country
it makes me so sad

My best friend Michael
when he went away
My house called The Villa
Where I used to play

Where do the lost things go
do you know?
Oh where do the lost things go?

When I was five,
I left my bike
and a toy called Smurfy
I really liked

My toys and my Lego
I misplaced them all
and that boy in my class
who was funny and tall

Where do the lost things go
do you know?
Oh where do the lost things go?

I lost an old photo
and my dragon called Krocky
Somewhere in my bedroom
Is my teddy called Lucky

I lost my old city
and my football team too
But since I came here
I've found new things to do.

And now I know the answer
All those things that I said -
They're not really lost...
They're still here, in my head!

world war 1

The Year 2014 marked one hundred years since the start of the First World War.

Year 6 wrote poems to remember that war (and all wars), and more importantly to think about peace.

WAR SHIP

Slowly day approaches night
Creepy crawlies are not a fright
The wars of day and night
All this fighting is not all right
Flashes of lightning we all hear
Pain in our heart throughout the year
Writing stories that can't be told

We will read them when the time has come
Though what they tell is not really the sum
Stepping through the treacherous mud
All the things that were never said
How many more days until the agony goes?
Maybe we'll know one day, for now…who knows?

Broken hope fills the room
Spreads like a pale skinned ghost, this gloom
100 words they never wrote
One hundred years can't fill the boat

by Rhianne

THE DAWN AND THE DUSK

The dawn and the dusk, the brave and afraid
The words that whisper to heaven in prayer
All the words within your mind
Watch them all, not one at a time
For they will go a far distance, like creatures lurking…
For this is not a rhyme.

Crying bitterly through the night
Words of wisdom, or are they fright?
Creeping up to creatures beyond
Staring sorrowfully through their soul
Then watch them all, not one at a time
Lives? Don't take them, for they are like stars
Once they are gone, they never return.

by Rhianne

THE WORDS OF WAR

Clouds of sadness
Pools of tears
Embers of sorrow

The words of war.

Depressing times
Piles of death
Abandoned hope

The Words of War.

Groups of isolation
Shelves of destruction
Walls of desperation

The words of war.

See the Poppies
In the fields
The soldiers souls
Are now the shields.

by Abbey

THE DARKNESS FALLS

The darkness falls, taking a life with it
A once stupendous place now turned to a sea of mud.
Each second taking a precious life with it
to the grave.

A flash of lightning and it's all over
Once great friends, now worst enemies.
Stuck in a pit of dismay until the end of time
metal, untamed beasts rampaging
for ever.

Darkness falls for ever, never ending.
I wish we would see dawn again.

by Sebastian

THE COLOUR OF RED

Poppies are red
So is Blood
Also Death
And also Love.

by Abbey

WHEN YOU'RE AWAY

When you're away I wonder
are you alive or hurt…but please
remember us and come back home.

WHEN YOU ARE GONE

I feel I was abandoned
please come back
and open presents with us.

THE GRASS

The grass was full of insects
but now it is all gone
now it is all gone.

There's no life on the fields
now it is all gone
all gone.

by Nadeer

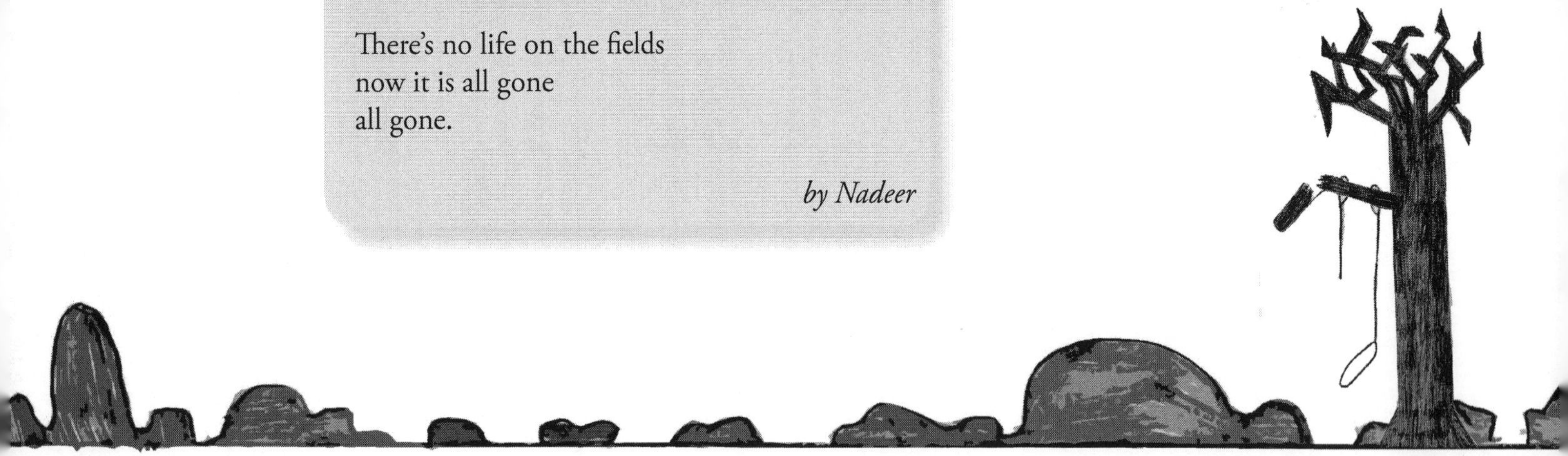

world war 2

WW2

Spit fire
ready to fire
ready to destroy
more lives.

Who can stop them?
Who can save us?
Was this meant to be?
Was this justice?

by Nickolas

WAR WITH THE PEOPLE

Occupation of the territory
React with the people
Leader of the war
Distract the hostile

Wild of the lion
Alarm of war
Real the war

Tactics of fight
Wolf aggressive
Obstacle by surpass.

by Victor

WORLD WAR 2!!

Misery and despair
that is all I see everywhere.
Ear piercing sounds petrify people,
a world with bombs to hear every night
does not deserve to be here.
But everyone has faith
everyone needs faith…

and what if our faith was shattered,
then what would happen?

by Christina

GUN SHOTS

Hearing gun shots everywhere
Everyone around me waiting
for the next big thing to happen.

Hiding myself behind a tree
Seeing everyone dying,
hearing people shouting loudly.

Just one big flash and then it's gone.

by Stephan

BOMB SHELLS

Bombshells still ringing in my ears
raid sirens scream like an alarm clock
waking me up in the night.

In this field of smoke, no man lives
the bang of guns is the only thing
that can be heard on the field of Death.

A silence falls at the end of battle.

Nothing is as devastating as War.

by Reece

THE SPIRAL OF WAR

The war went on for years, many people should know so today let us remember the war and the many more as this is a time to remember the war and rhyme.

by Reece

THESE THINGS WE SHOULD REMEMBER...

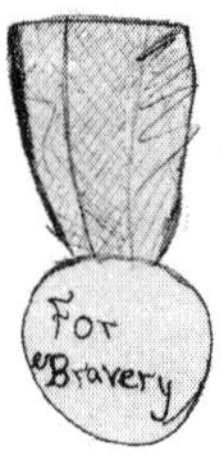

Worrying in fear
while the bomb strikes the floor.
Respect people
who died in the war.
Living in peace
watching people die.
Walking across the field,
dark as the night sky.
Obliterating people with airstrikes and guns
Resting in peace while the war ends.

by Jed

WORLD WAR 2 POEM

Smelling the thick smoky air
drifting through pale faces into soggy noses
echoes of deadly silence
quietly pass by skinny faces
staring into the emptiness.
Cold freezing air
brushes against my red pale cheeks.

by Hanan

WORLD WAR 2

Determination is what you need
If in war you want to succeed
So come on, be brave and bold
Pin to your heart those medals of gold
All that's inside should be strength and might
Hold to this tight to get through the night.

by Ferdows

WW2

Today the city
is nice and calm –
all day and all night
it's the place to be.

Today is boring
nothing to do
nothing to play,
I wish something would happen.

And now something has changed,
the city is no longer quiet.
There are bangs, crashes and booms
pinging day and night.

My mum has just told me
war has just started
I take back all I've said
but I can't change it now.

by Thara

WORLD WAR II POEM!

Hearing the bullets firing
as if a race has started.
Hiding behind my nation's tank
thinking what to do.

by Luka

My fearful heart
beating as fast
as the bullets shooting out

I was shocked
when I looked around
the sky as dark as a moon

This is a destroyed world
I feel so sleepy.

by Braw

A POEM FROM WORLD WAR 2 — THE TRUCE

Marching all day long, full of darkness and sorrow
and lots of pain in my heart
Everyone should know:
We're the best, We'll beat the rest…
We need a rest.
Walking through soft golden yellow sand
the Germans appeared on Christmas night.
We wanted to be with our families.
Holding my gun full of fear, too scared to say anything,
one of the Germans threw a ball.
We played together.
For one day we played football, shared cigarettes.
Showed each other pictures of our dear families.

The next day it was war again, *Have to kill for Britain*
No other choice, only sad darkness,
noises in my mind.

by Luisa

CLOUDS LIKE DARK SHADOWS

The clouds were like dark shadows
trying to capture me.
I knew that war was about to strike
its ear piercing sounds
of spitting bullets
were trying to fool me.
The heartbroken people like solemn ghosts
filled with indescribable emotion.
The menacing streets of Germany
trashed with once believed in homes.
But there was still hope which only one soldier knew.
He said, 'Why are we doing this?
Why don't we care?
Why are we fighting?
It's really not fair.'

by Lilla

POEM

The Germans invade
Britain declares war

The years of fighting
Will be four

They attack from the air
Oh what a scare!

Even the children have to fight
Britain and the Allies show their might

WWI is over as the enemies fall
We will never forget how war is cruel.

by Zoe

SORROW

Sadness.
People crying,
like rain drops.
Trees shining in the dust.
Bombs loud enough to make your ears explode.
People's backs are shivering, their bodies are shaking
in pain. People's power will never work if they don't try
hard enough. Their feelings are strong enough to make people die.
People put the blame on one another.

by Brenda

WORLD WAR 2

In 1945 everyone shouts for help
Children are dying, one dark night
WW2 begins and everyone's scared
all are depressed and fearful, frightened,
it's ghastly. Someone dies and we all
see the danger, everyone's creeping,
some countries unsafe and uncovered.
In this war we lose everything, our people.

by Taha

NEVER FORGET

Dark, gloomy and the foul stench of decay!
Sprinting and sprinting, they ran to get away.
Luscious green grass made my feet damp –
was it water, or was it what I think it was?

My life flashed before my eyes, I saw my best friend wounded, severely ill, could I help him? I hoped I would return to see my friends and family. Would I survive? Motionless, dispirited and close to dying, he told me to… *never forget.*

anon. (Yr 6)

THE STAGES OF WAR

Worried
Observation,
Ready to go to war.

Without food,
Hungry, tired.
Tired of fighting with people.

Children crying
People screaming
Pale faces, everyone is cold.

Light as the beautiful peace, dark as the blue dark water.

by Sindi

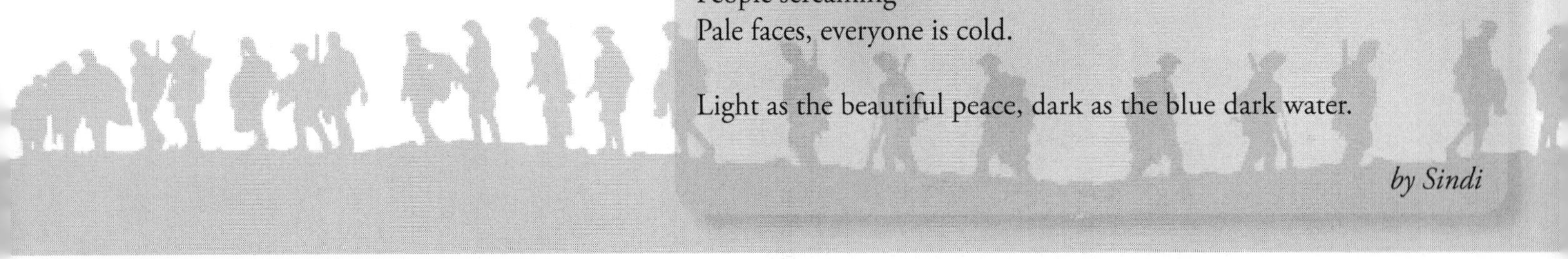

NOT THE SAME

Shining like a diamond in the sun,
bright rays glistened and shone.
The icy lake slipped into the horizon
like a sheet of pure, transparent glass.
Below the ice, fish swam playfully
in the sapphire blue water.
Meanwhile, birds swooped above
swirled like kites being carried
by the strong breeze
in the clear blue sky.
The glistening sun
looked like a giant beehive
floating in the sea -
its glowing honey
oozing out across the landscape.

It's not the same anymore…

Air raid sirens that shout and scream
give me headaches that are terrible.
They beat like a drum. On and on
and on they beat. Please stop!
I feel like my ears are bleeding…
the land, once green and lush
has turned into a brown,
blood-leaked mush.
What is there left for us?

My only wish is to survive –
is that too much to ask?
Still, if my wish backfires,
I would take death
and I would be happy.
I don't know what to do!
The water is undrinkable,
it's full of germs.
The germs make you catch
typhoid, cholera and chicken pox.

It's not the same anymore…

When will daddy come home? I want to see him now.
Is he dead already? I don't know how. He may be watching
over me but I know one thing for sure, he will live on
inside of me for I am his daughter, forevermore.

by Sammie

WISHING YOU HAD NEVER GONE

Poppies are red
so is blood
also death
and also love...

In no man's land

The stunned soldiers trudge
through sludge and slime
alone in a deep sea of misery
dodging bullets and fallen bodies

In no man's land

The boisterous bombs drop
around them like a heavy rain storm
suddenly arisen, an avalanche of thick
snow, a whirlwind of rough and cold

In no man's land

The guns spit bullets of death
an isolated shower of emptiness
in this field where nothing grows
a reaping of the cold hard end

In no man's land

The days close in, dawn breaks
too late, evenings come too early
The coldness creeps in slowly
soldiers emerge from the gloom

In no man's land

Coming home to emptiness
no one waiting for you there
Wishing you had never gone...
to no man's land.

by Abbey

WAR IS...

a sharp icicle in the chest,
the trembling at the back of your knees,
a dry mouth and a lump in the throat.

The German planes are popcorn machines,
the kind that no one has ever seen.

The treacherous sound of erupting bombs
is a song none of us can listen to for long.

Our people are gone within a flash
our homes are a pile of bricks and ash.

My heart has been split into four even pieces;
the earth, the ocean
and two children weeping.

by Lilla

THE HORRIFYING BLITZ

Hot-blooded fear
Afraid you will burst them out!

The bombs cry as they fall
from the sky.

The buildings tremble as
they break down.

The sky chokes on the thick
smoky air.

The sun hides his face in shame.

The night wraps herself in a blanket
full of holes.

No more good night!

by Sindi

war and peace

One of the ways we like to remember great achievements is by awarding prizes.

These next two poems on the subject of War and Peace were awarded First and Second Prize in a Creative Writing competition jointly organized by the participatory arts charity ReWrite, which aims to break down barriers of prejudice and racism through drama and creative writing, and the Wiener Library, the world's oldest Holocaust archive.

1ST PRIZE

DEATH—A CRIMINAL OF TERROR

Look into his eyes
Look at his sallow complexion
His eyes tearing up
blood gushing from his temple
Pain...

Flying shrapnel everywhere
Fire burning the memories away
Planes like wasps swarming
to protect their nests
Frightening...

Guns spitting bullets
Trees with naked limbs
Lifeless bodies
so quickly ripped to pieces
A vision of hell...

Taking his last breath,
Breathing heavily
like a horse on a cold morning
Saying his last words
I love you

by Saaqib (Yr 6)

2ND PRIZE

VISION OF HELL

Scary sirens scream
through the restless city,
as loud as Big Ben calling:

Terror!

Planes plunging forwards
through the misty night sky
taking flight like an evil witch

Horror!

Crumpled crackled earth –
will it ever grow again, or the newborn
baby, will we hear his first cry?

Speculation.

Burning bombs leaping overboard
glide through putrid smoky air
like a devastating angry tornado

Isolation.

Fierce flames spreading
through the old cobbled streets
like a deadly disease

Destruction!

Broken roads and buildings whimper
structures beyond repair
washed away by the tsunami of war

now...

Hope?

by Miki (Yr 6)

dreams

Sometimes we have dreams we'd like to remember and other times we have dreams we might prefer to forget.

Here is a poem written by eleven Year 6 children, all newly arrived at Highfield and learning to speak English. The poem imagines a Dreamgiver, the one who gives out all dreams, good or bad.

THE DREAMGIVER

Your name is Aloe
You are 100 years old
you are one million years old
you are ten million years old
You are happy, you are magical, you are scary
You live in a dream world
You give good dreams
Please, Aloe, I want…
Please make my dreams come true.
Thank you!

by Chris, Jordi, Nick S, Alex, Krasi, Brenda, Alejandra, Viki, Angelos, Vinamin and Sindi

black history month

During the month of October, children in Year 4 were looking specifically at the lives of important people from history with remarkable achievements, who often had to meet additional challenges due to prejudice and obstacles faced because of the colour of their skin.

The children were learning about Alice Marie Coachman (9th November 1923 – 14th July 2014), a famous American athlete and the first black woman to ever win an Olympic Gold medal.

Year 4 told Alice's story in haiku form:

THE STORY OF ALICE COACHMAN

Mornings with Grandma
Alice skipped ahead through fields
Born to run and jump

She vaulted over anything that got in her way

Papa told her, "Stop!"
Said she must cook, wash, do chores…
not sports with boys

She vaulted over anything that got in her way

Blacks did not have rights
Barefoot in dirt she high jumped
Soaring like a bird

She vaulted over anything that got in her way

Her talent notices
She left home and joined a team
Curious and shy

She vaulted over anything that got in her way

She ran like a flash
Brought food to hungry people
Tornadoes twisted

She vaulted over anything that got in her way

Moved to Tuskegee
special school for jumping high
she missed her family

She vaulted over anything that got in her way

Ice was thrown at her
Restaurants said 'Go away!'
World War II begun

She vaulted over anything that got in her way

College finished, she
kept training all the time through
dust, jogging… sprinting…

She vaulted over anything that got in her way

Finally her chance came
Jumping was painfully hard
but she had to win

She vaulted over anything that got in her way

Meeting new teammates
A long seven day voyage
dancing on the boat

She vaulted over anything that got in her way

War bombed streets, rubble
Always hungry, no water
London is too cold

She vaulted over anything that got in her way

Yes! The Olympics
Marching with both blacks and whites
Let the Games begin

She vaulted over anything that got in her way

Inch by inch higher
She's more and more determined
The King and Queen watched

She vaulted over anything that got in her way

The bar raised again
Alice focused on the jump
with hope in her heart

She vaulted over anything that got in her way

Her opponent jumped…
and missed. Now Alice's turn –
COACHMAN wins first place!

She vaulted over anything that got in her way

The first black woman
to have won a gold medal
The King was so proud

Alice Coachman, 1948 Olympic champion, vaulted over anything that got in her way

hospice project

For six weeks from November to December 2014, School Council members from Years 5 and 6 worked together with staff and patients from the North London Hospice on a project called **Remembering Through Words and Images,** to write poetry and make art.

We shared stories about our lives and important memories. We became buddies with those at the Hospice and got to know one another quite well. It was a lovely experience. These are some of the poems we created together to tell those stories.

OUR UTOPIA OF REMEMBERED PLACES

The view of London beneath your feet
Chilly, but refreshing.
Memories in the garden, remembering…
a trip to Uganda, home in Tunisia, a holiday on Holcombe Beach
in North Norfolk, being at the park…
Do you know, I counted 500 planes on D-Day -
seeing the eagles flying through the sky was magical
…Feel the sand between your toes,
warm and nice and soft
See the azure sea, the azure sky,
smell the ozone
at the top of a monument on Fish Hill.
Purple beds
feeling relaxed and happy
The living room is the heart of the home
Relaxed and comfortable.
Freedom,
the experience of a lifetime
somewhere to
belong.

by (from Highfield) Ferdows, Joseph, Khushi, Lina, Sebastian, Ahsen, George, Christina, Cheryl and Helen (from North London Hospice) Rod, Robert, Mark, Toni, Terry, Laurence, Graham, Betty, Tim, Heather, and Karen

The patients at the Hospice told the children at Highfield about the things, places and people that are most special to them, and the children helped the patients to write cinquains about these things so that they could be kept as treasured memories.

A holiday photo taken at the seaside:

Photo
Family and friends
Higgledy, piggledy
Big majestic castle of sand
Picture

A favourite walking place in the Peak District:

Dovedale
Valleys and hills
Walking in the beauty
Happiness is all around me
Dovedale

A treasured present given to a young girl by her father:

Topsy
Sweet little mouth
Loved birthday gift
Makes me smile with good memories
My doll

A cherished and much missed wife (and the watch she left behind):

Shirl's watch
Gold, clear and slim
Went far, never mislaid
You'd better take this home with you…
Heartbeat

Shirley
My pretty girl
gentle, tender, caring
You could have been the Queen's double
Duchess

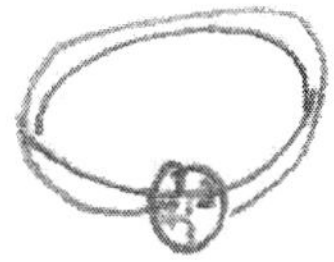

Proud memories of a career as a boxer:

Round 1 –
Boxing
Thousands watching
The battle commences
3rd round win, victory is sweet
Wembley

Round 2 –
Bell goes
Straight in the ring
Red shorts with tassles, few bevvies…
They say I roll with the punches
Rolling Roy

Grateful for technology and the connections it enables:

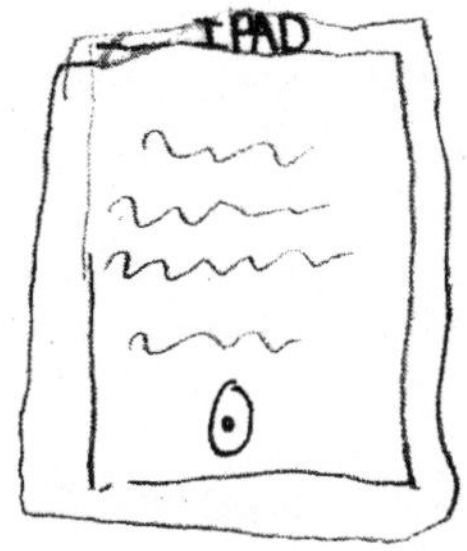

Ipad
Lots of fab apps
One touch to chat with friends
Waiting to see smiling faces
Happy

Many of us had never been in a Hospice before. We discovered it to be a lovely place that we looked forward to coming back to week after week.

We wanted to let others know what we had discovered.

GROUP CINQUAIN ON HOSPICE

(and all the ideas that led to it...)

suntrap - happiness - care - welcoming - calming oasis - comforting - blanket - welcome roofgarden - sharing - reassurance - bright and lovely - belonging - togetherness - helpful - support friendship - pain relief - warmth - nature friendly - quiet garden - lovely in the summer - palliative friendly - relaxation - place to relax - unique - delicious - companionship - working together colourful - friendly - welcome - unique - helpful companionship - deliciously helpful

Hospice
Warm and lovely
Helpful companionship
Sunbeams shine with joyful laughter
Happy

dali class

DALI Class made up a story about being trapped inside the stomach of a dinosaur. Luckily the story has a happy ending. This is their poetry version of that story.

IN THE BELLY OF A T-REX

Way down in the T-Rex tummy
It is dark and creepy.

Sticky and icky, cold and scary
Rumbly, grumbly noises.

When the dragon comes he breathes
Red and blue and yellow fire.

It is hot and burning, burning hot
Breathing fire, sizzle, crackle, choking.

The water in the well is cold and splashy
Splashy and dripping.

Cools you down
Swimming free!

by Issabelle (Yr 1), Abby (Yr 2), David (Yr 3), Tyrell (Yr 2), and Ellis (Rec)

anti-bullying month

November was ANTI-BULLYING month, although at Highfield we think it's important to be anti-bullying all year round.

BULLIES ARE A VIRUS

Bullies are a virus,
bystanders are minus
heartbreaking words
all of the bad words…
cries of pain.

Names that hurt, kicks, punches and flicks, threats overpowering you

Don't be nasty…

Say NO to bullying!!!

Follow the rules
don't stay behind in school
Just because of bullying
Mean words can hurt you bad

SAY NO TO BULLYING!!!!

by Rhianne (Yr 6)

DON'T BE BULLIED

Being bullied is like being in a prison,
frightened and cold
When the bullies are rude
the lightning strikes at you.

Don't be bullied! Don't do wrong!
Just because the bullies are strong

Remember, you are a brick wall
where everything else is stone and dust –
you can't be broken.

Don't be bullied! Don't be weak!
Just because the bullies are peak!

by Kaan (Yr 5)

THEY'RE FAKE

They have a gang of bullies
To make them feel strong
They're fake, they're fake, they're fake
and you know to make them shake
The others, they are fake, fake fake
and you know they're nothing.
Just believe in yourself
cos you know you're not the only one
in this mayhem
but then again…
Hot like a fire with a bitter taste
Mmhmm… just a hollow brick wall.

by No Bullies Allowed a.k.a. Emileo (Yr 5)

WHY BE A BULLY?

Why be a bully, just be you
Just be me

Has he looked in the mirror
eyes bursting in tears

Make sure you're a friend
Not a bully

Don't be acting tough
When you're not

Has he looked in the mirror
eyes bursting in tears

Just be me
Be yourself.

by Ollie & Suber (Yr 5)

LIKE A BULLY

Bullies, bullies, they're fast like a trolley
Looking for stuff then letting go, go

Bitter taste, then aftertaste

You think you've gotten rid but then you see the next kick
It happens every time and you know what it's like
But you have no courage left to do what you should do, do

Bullies, Bullies, they are only loonies
Pushing to the ground then letting go, go

by Jackson (Yr 5)

SORRY

(inside the mind of a bully)

People hate me.
To them I'm like a rash –
one that never goes away.
I harass them every day
When they play
I end their fun
I drive them mad
It seems like my goal
is to make them sad
It's jealousy that runs my engine
and this is the only thing that makes me feel better.

You're a bully, so are they!
You go home, far away.
Bursting in tears
OK… okay!
Black and white
it's just not right
bruised and blue
it could be you

So yes, this is my story
It's the only way I can say sorry.

by Joseph (Yr 5)

PLEASE

Please don't be mean
Please don't be mean
I'm just a lonely person
Please don't bully me

It's just not right
Boo hoo, boo hoo
Now I must be strong
to stand up to you

You were the same as me
Just leave me alone
Let me be
Please, Please, PLEASE!

What's your point
There is no need to fight
If you stop now
You'll feel all right

You know what I mean
Just rise above the mean
To be rude and disrespectful is a crime
So please stop Mr. Bully
Please just stop this time.

Do you bully because you are bullied?
If you just got strong
why not be strong and just?

Just stand up and be a better person.
Please, please, please… Be a better person.

by Suber (Yr 5)

Everyone in the school drew round the shape of their foot and wrote important statements about themselves inside their own footprint. We called these our 'Dream Slippers' and placed them around the walls of the school - a way of letting someone else walk for a while in our shoes.

I am a smiley face
I know how to play table tennis
I want to play better at table tennis
I believe you can't judge a book by its cover
One day I will become a famous table tennis player

I am a snake
I know how to play video games
I want to be better at beat boxing
I believe in destiny
I will be a Sledgehammer games worker

I am a teddy
I know how to play
I want to improve my skills
I believe in destiny
One day I will become a chef

I am a jet black stallion
I know dance is freedom
I want to be happy
I believe everyone can achieve
One day I will become mindful

I am a bright gold brick,
I know how to play football
I want to become better for my football team
I believe you can't judge a book by its cover
One day I will become a footballer

I am a gold rose
I know how to cook
I want to be a better singer
I believe everyone is equal
One day I will be a doctor

I am a cheetah
I know how to debate
I want to improve my Maths
I believe in second chances
One day I will be a billionaire

I am a fun book
I know I am a good football player
I want to be better at Maths
I believe in God
One day I will be a perfect footballer

I am a giggly bubble
I know about fashion styles
I want for people to always have a smile on their face
I believe that no one is different!
One day I will become a lawyer

I am a thorny rose
I know how to play games
I want to improve my literacy
I believe life is a book; there's a beginning and an end
One day I will become a programmer

I am an iPhone
I know I am good in art
I want an animal
I believe in my future
One day I will be a vet

I am an ice cube
I know how to party
I want to get a higher level
I believe in God
One day I will be a famous singer

I am a painted musical note
I know how to play instruments
I want to be better at science
I believe life is an honour
One day I will become a professional violin player

I am a snake
I know slithering my way out of trouble
I want to beat my brother at Monopoly
I believe life is a cupboard, it opens and closes
One day I'll be a CIA cop with my brother

I am a shy little fox
I know I am good at cooking
I want to be better at art
I believe in true friendship
One day I will be a stylist

I am an innocent flower
I know how to dance and knit
I want to be better at Maths and English
I believe everyone is beautiful in a way
One day I will be a doctor

I am a beautiful hot fire
I know how to make tea and coffee
I want to be a better singer
I believe there is no god
One day I will be a teacher

I am fair
I know how to play Minecraft
I want to get better at English
I believe life has just begun
One day I will be a millionaire

I am a smile
I know how to write a song
I want all the world to be together
I believe music is magic
One day I will be a popular song writer

I am a monkey
I know how to do dancing
I want to learn to beatbox better
I believe that people are reborn
One day I will be a celebrity

TREAD SOFTLY

Poem for Anti-Bullying Month

If you stepped into my shoes
for just one moment you would be
close to understanding
what it is that makes me, me

You'd have a glimpse of who I am
instead of how I seem;
what I know... I want... believe in –
you'd even know my dreams!

I am a jet black stallion
a painted musical note
a strong but elegant lion
a book that no one wrote

I'm a cheetah, red hot fire
I'm a brick, a hug, a bubble
I'm a smile, I'm a monkey
a snake slithering out of trouble

I'm an ice cube, I'm an iPhone
refreshing, and I'm smart
I'm good at cooking, dancing
football, I'm even good at art!

I'm a shy fox, I'm a flower
I am a golden thorny rose
I am funny, I am shiny
I'm a secret no one knows

I know that dancing equals freedom
I know that music can be magic
I know that time flies by too quickly
So to waste it is just tragic

I believe in second chances
and that together we achieve
I value friendship and forgiveness
That's what I believe

I think life is like a cupboard
doors open and they shut
understanding keeps them open
but bullying does not

If you stepped into my shoes
for just one moment you would be
close to understanding
what it is that makes me, me!

Cheryl Moskowitz

THE CHILD WHO ASKED

A small child who didn't know what words meant
came to me and asked,
"What is bullying?"

I told the child,

Bullying is a scar in the skin,
Bullying is a rough sea clashing against the rocks
Bullying is a cracked window,
a dent in your shiny new toy car.
Bullying is a hole in our heart.

Then the child asked,
"But what is a bully?"

Err… hmm… it's hard to explain

A bully is a bit like a big chocolate bunny
with high proud whiskers
and a shiny gleaming wrapper
and when you peel back the foil
there is dark yummy chocolate…
but when you take a bite
it's hollow inside.

The child's big eyes that were like round china plates
and the child's rosy face like a big red balloon
cracked and deflated
into a pile of soft rose petals
scattered round the room.

Don't worry my child,
the world is wide
choose your path and the words you will use –

You don't have to be a bully
You can be jolly
You don't have to have clashing
You can have kindness
You don't have to have rough seas
You can have respect
Turn scars into care
Cracks and dents
into friendship
and the holes in our hearts
into love.

Come with me…
Together we can achieve more!

by Alex (Yr 6) and Cheryl

new year

The Autumn term is long and seemingly endless – so much can happen in the space of those four months, September, October, November, December – but before you know it, the leaves have all gone from the trees and the holidays are upon us.

After the holidays is the start of a new school term and the beginning of a brand new calendar year...

NEW YEAR POEM FOR HIGHFIELD

Pass it on said Autumn to Winter.
Whisper so that Spring won't hear
... Summer is too far off to care.

There's something different in the air
The gold-red coat trees used to wear
has become white sparkle everywhere.

September's over, October's through
November, December, they're done too
This year that's here is all brand new.

Janus, the God of gates and doors
Waves goodbye to all befores
It's fresh beginnings he adores.

Beginnings always follow ends
So pass this on to all your friends
By word of mouth or with your pen,

Happy New Year to everyone!

Cheryl Moskowitz

creation story

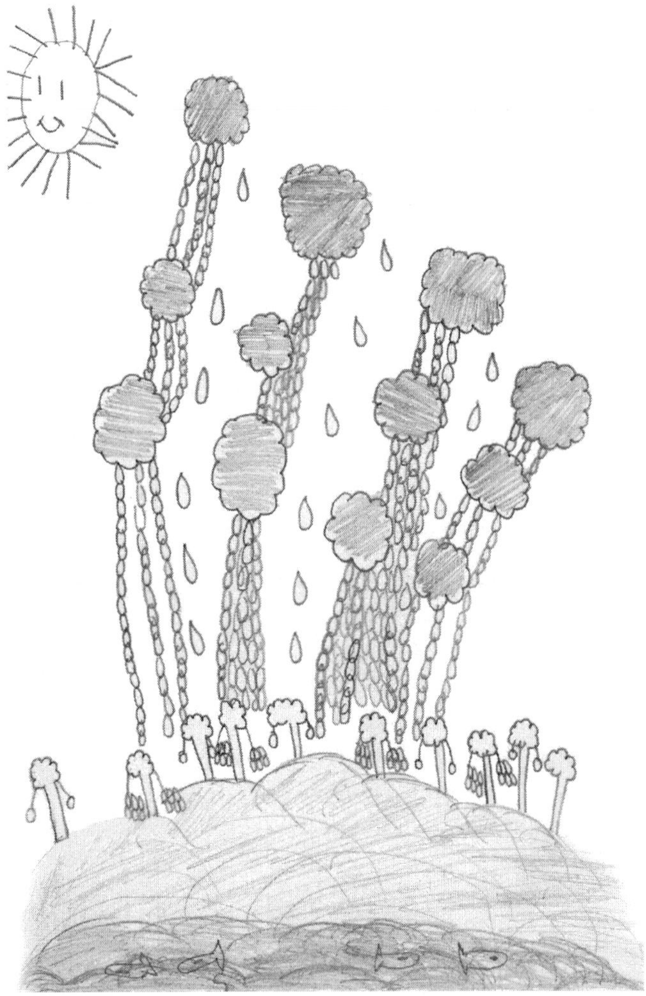

In January Highfield held a Religious Education week and every class in the school was learning about the Creation Story.

Here are three versions of the Christian creation story, retold as poems by Year 1.

CREATION STORY

First there was nothing,
silent, dark nothing
empty nothing,
nothing there
blank.

Then there was light
shiny hot light
bright sunlight
sparkly
light.

Then there was water
popping, plopping rainwater
wavy seas, running rivers
reflecting lakes
shiny
water.

Then there was land
tall trees, colourful leaves and flowers
yellow daffodils, dandelions, and
sunflowers,
green apples, pears and squishy bananas
tasty
food.

Then God made sky
fluffy white clouds
curved bright moon
pointy stars like twinkly diamonds
sparkling
heavens.

Then came creatures
fish, grasshoppers, mice
eagles, elephants, scary tigers
fast cheetahs, white furry rabbits
and a stripy zebra.
Beautiful.

Finally God made people,
Nice, kind, friendly and helpful
Friends, family, healthy and happy
clever
people

Then, God took a nap.

GOD'S WORLD STORY

In the beginning it was pitch black
Completely blank
You couldn't see anything

So God used his magical powers
He made daylight to go with the night
It was summery, sunny, bright, sparkling and shiny

Then God made water
Pouring down, splashing into puddles
Lightning cracking the air

Then he put silver stars in the sky
like jewels sparkling about, and a golden shiny moon
Sometimes round like a circle and sometimes curved like a crescent

On the fifth day he made bushes, trees and flowers
Tall trees, fat with leaves of rainbow colours
Flowers with soft petals, yellow dandelions, red roses, pink and purple posies

God wanted to display his beautiful work
So he made animals; furry lions that roar and fluffy cats that meow
And at the end he made the girls and boys, he made us!

Finally God had a stretch, a mighty yawn
He rubbed his eyes, looked around at the world and before he rested
He said, 'This is great, this is gorgeous, this is golden and this is good.'

IN THE BEGINNING

In the beginning
There was nothing but God and darkness
Then he magicked the sun into the sky
and the sun was… bright
and the sun was… shiny
and the sun was… yellow
and the sun was… hot
And when it was sunny it was Day
and when the sun went to bed it was Night.

On the second day
God (because he was thirsty) made water
and the water was… wavy and wet
and the water was… beautiful, clear and soft
and the water was… cold, clean and fresh
and the water was… healthy and delicious
And when God saw it he knew it was fantastic
And when God drank it he knew it was good.

We discovered that there are as many different ideas about how the world began as there are children at Highfield School.

Year 5 wrote a poem that encapsulated just about everything.

OUR CREATION STORY

In the beginning there was a bang
A blinding flash of light.
It lit up the shadows.

In the beginning there was a tornado of rocks hitting each other
They made one giant rock
Then God made the world

In the beginning there were two fireballs
They collided and exploded into the colours of earth
The colours found their way into creation

In the beginning there was fire
Fire, volcanoes and ashes on earth
The volcanoes erupted like a kettle boiling water

In the beginning was a magical fire
a volcano of nature
The volcano erupted and forests grew

In the beginning there was a magical red fire
God made the fire collide with an empty planet
There was a big explosion and that's when life started.

In the beginning there was a magical red fire
The flame roamed the earth and transformed into a Lion
The Lion called all the animals together to help him build

In the beginning there was a big bang
All the elements crashed together creating the first human
God gave the human a choice.

In the beginning there was a giant blob of clay
It separated into two smaller pieces
The humans, Adam and Eve, were created

In the beginning there was Adam and Eve
They found a mighty tree with a holy apple growing on it
Adam took it and ate it and more grew

In the beginning was a teardrop
The teardrop fell into a magical pond and made Adam and Eve
Adam and Eve made the beautiful world

In the beginning there was a teardrop
The teardrop dropped onto the ground
And created the ocean!!

In the beginning was a giant volcano
The volcano erupted
When the lava cleared the first blade of grass was visible.

In the beginning there was a single blade of grass
The grass grew bigger and longer and became a grass hand
The hand made fire and water crash together, it was a beautiful earth.

In the beginning there was a tree
A leaf fell out of the tree and transformed into a hand
The hand was God's hand

In the beginning there was a leaf floating in the air
The colourful leaf fell in the water
The leaf exploded and the darkness came apart!

In the beginning there was a giant blob of black clay
The clay hardened into the ground and burst into pieces
A starburst that created the world and everything

In the beginning was a dark pathway gazing at me
The pathway led to the magical land of light
There I saw trees and branches

In the beginning there was a magical drawer
God opened his magic drawer and threw the stars in
The planet earth was created

In the beginning was a giant egg
The egg hatched with an almighty crack
Two people stepped out and created the family that made the world!

In the beginning there was one tiny egg
The egg hatched into air and stardust
The dust landed softly and became life

In the beginning there were tall green trees
A drop of water fell on a tree and turned into a troll
A tear dropped from the troll's eyes and created a baby boy.

In the beginning was Minecraft
Then there was the world
Then there was stardust and people

In the beginning there was God
Then there was a big light
A new baby opened its eyes and made the whole entire universe

go Highfield!

At Highfield we have four school teams, the Reds, the Blues, The Yellows and the Greens. These teams lead the way in sports, Comic Relief, and raising money for charities.

Team Captains are elected to represent their teams. Team Captains can be poets too. At Highfield they certainly are!

A team poem can be a great way of rallying the troops.

TEAM POEMS

RALLY FOR THE REDS

We are the reds
racing is our game
rallying responsibility
respect is our name
Reds Rule!!

GREEN TEAM INGREDIENTS

Try your best and take part,
Behave!
Show respect, teamwork and forgiveness
Cooperation!
Be careful , be kind to each other and look after the environment
and finally
Don't Give Up!!!

TEAM YELLOW

Say hello
Be good fellows
Always follow
Your loyal Yellows

Remember your mates
Cheer them on
Remember your captain
When he's gone

BLUE TEAM

treats, trips and celebrations
teamwork to get more team on team tournaments
cooperate, work together, be respectful, artistic, creative
Blue sky thinking…

by Yr 6 Team Captains: Abbey and Isobella (Red), Kieran and Nadeer (Yellow) Dever and Masheed (Green), Misbah and Ja'lan (Blue)

The Team Captains are also responsible for selling red noses and encouraging fund-raising for charities on Comic Relief's Red Nose Day.

POETRY SLAM FOR RED NOSE DAY 13TH MARCH 2015

RED TEAM

Don't provoke the smoke
Smoke is not a joke

Smelly drains and rattling bins
A little cash can change everything

Cleaner toilets, cleaner roads
Cleaner houses can help them loads

Alleyways full of rubbish,
Houses falling down
Waste covering the city streets
Smoke smothering the town

Don't provoke the smoke
Smoke is not a joke

So please donate on Red Nose Day…
Just one pound and we'll all say HOORAY!!!!

by Abbey (Yr 6) and Isobella (Yr 6)

GREEN TEAM

Hungry with no cash, turns your hopes to ash -
Rumbling tummies are not very funny!!

People alone,
no friends, no home
Never fear
Comic Relief is here.

You may be on the street, nearly dead
Or lying in a hospital bed…
I'll tell you a joke to cheer you up:

What do you call a homeless fish?
A sea urchin!

You have a place on earth like them (and any other person)
Comic Relief is your friend!!

by Dever (Yr 6) and Rhianne (Yr 6)

BLUE TEAM

Help! Help! There are people dying.
Don't leave the sick and the poorly crying.
If you give money, their faces will be sunny
and the world will be as sweet as honey!!

Help! Help! Save them all.
We can do it, us boys and girls.

There goes the money around the world...

For people in hospital beds
For people who are nearly dead.

by Misbah (Yr 6) and Ja'lan (Yr 6)

YELLOW TEAM

Paper and pens, pencils and books
and a good ruler... can change everything!!!

Paper and pens are all like gold
A treasure that can't be bought or sold
We have loads and they have none
They have a right to read and learn.

Paper and pens, pencils and books
and a good ruler... can change everything!!!

Everyone needs a good ruler
That could be Highfield boys and girls
Let's not be stuck and stationary
Let's give stationery to the world!

by Miki (Yr 6) and Nadeer (Yr 6)

poetry surgery

At lunchtimes, as often as I could, I ran a poetry surgery for anyone who wanted to have some extra time and space for writing their own poems.

A group of girls from Year 3 were regular Poetry Surgery attenders and they also wrote a poem to perform on Red Nose Day, just in case anyone was still wondering what Comic Relief is all about.

WHO KNOWS WHAT A RED NOSE IS FOR?

So shiny it makes my eyes burst
like the golden sun
From Funnyland I could put it into a comedy
Makes me smile
like my baby cousin when he makes a gurgling sound
Reminds me of people
who don't have everything they need in life
food… drink… clothes… medicine...
Makes us think about what we have
and be grateful for it.
I wear my red nose
so that I know
and you know
and everyone knows
What a red nose is for.

by Ayla, Ascari, Iman, Mia, and Qadijo

world book day

In March we also celebrated World Book Day. Years 3 and 4 thought about the sort of books they like to read and and where they like to read them and imagined the books they might write one day themselves.

WORLD BOOK DAY POEM 5TH MARCH 2015

Take a look
inside this book
we love to read

In this book,
you will see
there will be...

Nature Imagination Adventure, Stars, Strength, Destiny
Family, Friendship, Blessings, Freedom, Love, Home,
Life

The Magic Forest… flowers and grass,
a waterfall that smells like a jungle

a fresh green field with lovely flowers
a beautiful sunrise and birds singing

you will taste the happiness of birds
blue birds and white doves.

Take a look
inside this book
we love to read

In this book,
you will see
there will be...

A journey… to the stars and moon, the planets
meteors flying past, a space adventure

a cheese eating mouse
in a cheese eating house

A beach by the hot sea… seagulls, seashells, tropical fish
ice cream, hot dogs, salt on your lips

A kingdom called Justice Town… a knight, a horse,
a victor
crashes and bangs, explosions, dust everywhere

A secret garden, a dance kingdom, a mind word tree
a talking jungle, a magical marble, a whispering sea
A place in Dinosaurs' time… a lake, fresh plants,
cool wind
Komodo dragons in the desert breathing fire

Take a look
inside this book
we love to read

In this book,
you will see
there will be...

Darkness and silence… nothingness,
thoughts and feelings, destiny

A family laughing, a girl called Luna
an aeroplane flying to Greece and New York

There will be colourful sea pearls, starfish and ponies,
fizzy pop, families with fortunes and stolen money

You will taste the happiness of home
strawberry ice-cream and chocolate cake

Come inside
this place I hide
my book and me

Let me show
you where I go
when I read.

I read in a car, on the bus or the train
I read in the mosque, high up in a plane

I read in a tree, on a bike, in a cave, at the circus
I read near a blue waterfall next to some flowers

I read on the head of a diamond in a giant's hand
I read in a crystal mansion in a faraway land

I make my own den and I read in there
I read on the beach sitting in a deck chair

I read in the library and in the reading shed
I read to my friends and I read in my head

I read in the classroom, I read in the park
I read under the covers, in the dark

I read in a tree house and up in the clouds
Sometimes I read silently, sometimes out loud

I read on a ship in the ocean under the sun
I read in the living room on the sofa with Mum

I read sitting on top of the lions at Trafalgar Square
To be honest I like to read everywhere!

World Poetry Day was also in March. In Reception we thought that if the whole world was thinking about poetry we should be thinking about the world, and write about it in a poem. We thought about the sky, the sea, and the land. On the day before World Poetry Day there was a solar eclipse and the sun disappeared behind the moon. We put that in our poem too.

POETRY IS IN OUR WORLD. LET'S PUT OUR WORLD INTO A POEM!!

Listen to the sounds of the sky
You can hear the wind blowing…
You can hear the wind whistling…
You can hear the wind howling…
You can hear the wind waving
to the planet Jupiter –
Garimela!!

On the planet Jupiter, it is HOT!!
From the planet Jupiter we can see Mars
On the planet Mars there are aliens –
Du La Lu!

From the planet Mars we can see
China… *Ni Hao!*
Africa… *As-salamu alaykum*
Jamaica… *Ciao Ciao*
and from the tops of the trees we can see
the birds, the bees
and the butterflies in the branches
blowing in the breeze

T-wit t-woo
T-wit t-woo
Bzzz Bzzz

twinkle twinkle
like the stars
near Mars
in the sky
where the sun
is hiding today
behind the moon.

POETRY IS IN OUR WORLD.
LET'S PUT OUR WORLD INTO A POEM!!

In our world there is water
Water can be blue
Water can be green
Water can be see-through
Through water we see everything!

Listen to the sounds of water
Even water can be wet!

Goo goo goo goo… goo goo goo
pitter patter pitter patter
whoosh, whoosh
splish splash splish splash
glug glug glug glug
drip drop drip drop
Water can be blue
Water can be green
Water can be see-through
Through water we see everything!

Jelly fish are pink, we think!
They swim underwater and sometimes they sting… OW!

Squids are squidgy
and they stink, we think!
If you touch them, they move
And they might even bite! …OW!

Listen to the sounds of water
Even water can be wet!

Goo goo goo goo… goo goo goo
pitter patter pitter patter
whoosh, whoosh
splish splash splish splash

glug glug glug glug
drip drop drip drop

Water can be blue
Water can be green
Water can be see-through
Through water we see everything!

POETRY IS IN OUR WORLD.
LET'S PUT OUR WORLD INTO A POEM!!

Listen to the sounds on earth. People talking…
in French, *Bonjour!*
in English, *Hello!*
in Reception… *Wala Wala, Wala*

Children playing, shouting to their friends
Come and play with me
Come and play
Come and play…it's fun!
LET'S PLAY!!!

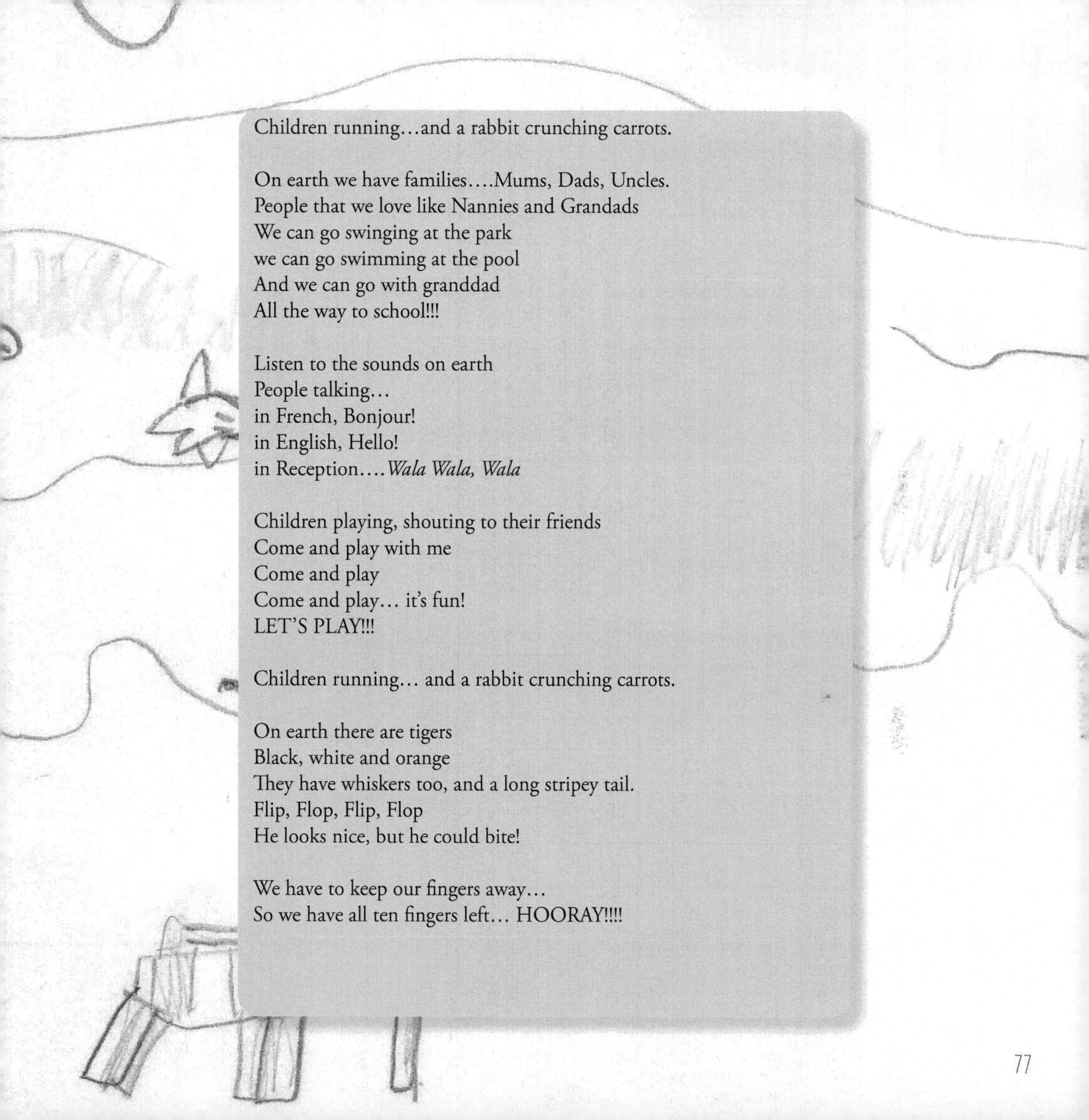

Children running…and a rabbit crunching carrots.

On earth we have families….Mums, Dads, Uncles.
People that we love like Nannies and Grandads
We can go swinging at the park
we can go swimming at the pool
And we can go with granddad
All the way to school!!!

Listen to the sounds on earth
People talking…
in French, Bonjour!
in English, Hello!
in Reception….*Wala Wala, Wala*

Children playing, shouting to their friends
Come and play with me
Come and play
Come and play… it's fun!
LET'S PLAY!!!

Children running… and a rabbit crunching carrots.

On earth there are tigers
Black, white and orange
They have whiskers too, and a long stripey tail.
Flip, Flop, Flip, Flop
He looks nice, but he could bite!

We have to keep our fingers away…
So we have all ten fingers left… HOORAY!!!!

poems can be about anything

Poems can be written about anything, at any time. You never know when you are going to be inspired so it is a good idea to carry around a notebook and a pencil just in case an idea comes to you.

Here are a few poems that were written that way by children at Highfield. Spontaneous poems that just appeared on my desk or were thrust into my hand excitedly by young poets who knew they had just written something special and needed someone else to see it. And I'm so glad they did!

TOWER BRIDGE

Tower Bridge is oh so strong
The hydraulics work all day long
Underneath the deep blue Thames
Tall ships glide across to the other end

by Tobias (Yr 1)

WHAT IS IT?

What is that bright light?
Could it be a star?
Could it be a car?
Will it come closer?
Or will it go back?
Could it be a thing, or someone?
I really don't know
because it's dark
and all I can see is the moon.

by DeJhaun (Yr 3)

THE 4 SEASONS

Summer is a shiny and lovely season
the children are as cute as so many puppies
as they come out and play with their suddenly not-so-strict parents.

Spring is a blooming season
when flowers grow to the sky
but here's a secret… summer is better!

Autumn is the death of leaves as they fall
to make a carpet on the ground so you can jump and jump
until the wind comes and sends them to heaven.

Winter is as cold as seven seas
makes you want to sail away on the ice and make a snowman
or stay inside and have hot cocoa and soup to warm you up.

I will whisper my secret again…
Winter is cold, Spring is lovely, Autumn is better, but not like summer!

by Antonia (Yr 4)

WHATEVER THE WEATHER

I don't mind
Sun I love
rain I hate
cold I hate
storms I hate
I love weather!

by Christian (Yr 1)

I AM…

I am Mr. Chocolate Cake
I am Mr. Yummy Spoonful
I am Mr. Busy
I am Mr. Paper
I am Mr. Plate
I am Mr. Piggy Bank

the end

by Christian (Yr 1)

PITTER PITTER PAT

On a cold Sunday morning
The sun is awake, yawning
Young Johnny heard something outside
He got up to his brother Clyde

He said *pitter pitter pat…*
What is that?
The Ocean could be falling on us.
Clyde just ignored
because he was bored
so Johnny went to his mum
"Can you come," he asked,
"with me outside?
No one will listen to me,
not even Clyde."

He said *pitter pitter pat…*
What is that?
Water is falling on us.

Mum couldn't hear
she was making dinner
She made it healthy
so Johnny would get thinner

He went to his sister, Kelly
Who he liked to call 'Smelly'

and he said *pitter pitter pat…*
What is that?
The Ocean has fallen on us.

He asked his sister,
and he asked his brother.
No one would listen,
not even his mother.

Then he asked
his good friend Wayne
Wayne answered,
"Johnny, it's rain."

Johnny thanked him again and again
and waved goodbye to his good friend Wayne.

by Reece (Yr 6)

SET ME FREE

Someone help me
set me free
I'm being blamed for something
that was not me.
But no one came
to rescue me
so I think to myself...
I think to myself...
all the words I can grab
and make them a rap
I beg you please
to listen to these
Imagine
Imagine
Let your mind see
Your imagination
can set me free.

by Qadijo (Yr 3)

MY FAVE-WRITE POEM

Poems are full of ideas
they make pictures in your head
when you read or hear them
oceans crashing, ponds sweet flowing
rhythm and rhymes with noises
that rise to a cold wildness.

by Qadijo (Yr 3)

MABEL

My nan is a part of me
that will never release.
A token of her love
is the ring she left me.
Our strong connection
could never end.
The day she left
was the day I believed
I would soon meet
her again.
Her love
still lives
in me.

by Rhianne (Yr 6)

SPECIAL MEMORIES OF MY BFF

My BFF is very sweet
She's not so keen on maths or PE like me
It doesn't matter, because she's not me
She is special and she is she.
She might not know a lot of things
but she understands and inspires me.

by Abbey (Yr 6), Isobella (Yr 6)

reception poems

Some very keen young writers in Reception presented me with these gems.

ROYAL

The Queen has a crown
The princess has a tiara
The crown is sparkly
The tiara has diamonds

by Sofia

NATURE

The sky is blue
The grass is green
says some people,
the people that are sad.
We know you can
dry your eyes
and you can
be happy.

by Alice

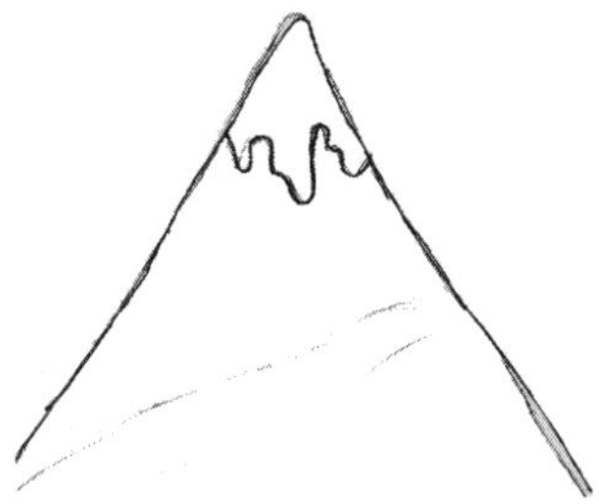

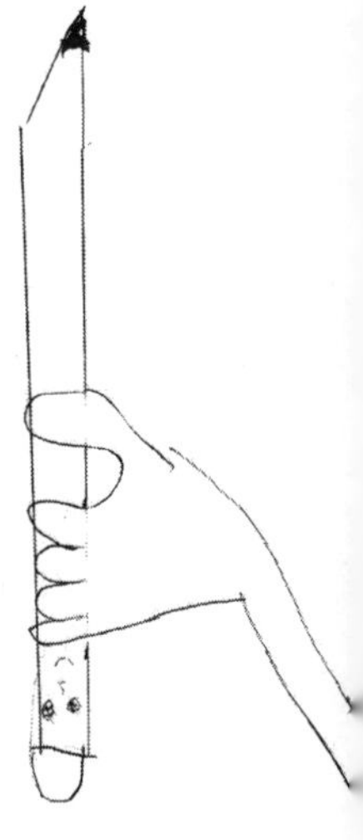

OCEAN POEM

I can see four fish
in the sea
I see the sea
I like the sea
the fish are yellow
the fish are dark
the sea is warm
the sea is blue
the shell is beautiful
I see a crocodile.

by Lexi

DRAGONS

Dragons
are bad
and blow
lightning bolts

by Charlie

ISLAND

The sky is blue
The grass is green
The chair is wiggly
The mountains are high
The whole island is great
The fruit is nice to eat

by Suden

‘everybody has won…’

"Everybody has won and all must have prizes."
(The Dodo Bird verdict from *Alice's Adventures in Wonderland* by Lewis Carroll)

Writing a poem is always an achievement but it's sometimes good to have a particular target - a deadline - a reason to polish up your poem and make it the best it can possibly be.

Of course, there is no right or wrong in poetry but there are always going to be some poems (our own or someone else's) that we think are better than others.

The following poems were all written for competitions - school, local, and national - over the course of the year. Some of these poems were awarded prizes by the judges. In my opinion, they are all winners.

THE JOURNEY HOME

Stomping across the blanket of leaves
A crinkle here, a crinkle there
A soft gentle breeze

Families of birds soaring up in the sky
The clouds like soft feathery pillows
Swaying in the wind, the tall slender willows

Trees like people
Their branches reaching out to keep me warm
Remembering the hugs they gave me

Nearly there…to my family.

by Zahra (Yr 5)

THE GOLDEN SUN

The golden sun rises like a flying bird
When it gets there it will make me shiver.

The golden sun stays till as a mouse
It never moves till it goes down.

When the sun sets the sky turns pink
And it will make me think.

When the sun goes, we lose our things
Because it is so very dark.

The golden sun, bright as fire
It shines too bright but to me, it is no matter.

by Amelia (Yr 4)

WAITING WAITING

Sitting in the classroom
with nothing to do

waiting, waiting

for our new teacher
to come into the room

waiting, waiting

Would this teacher be kind?
Would this teacher be a beast?
Would this teacher be bold
and have rabbit-like teeth?

waiting, waiting

Would this teacher have pointy ears
and come from Pontefract?
Or would this teacher teach us how to rap?

waiting, waiting

Would this teacher be cool
or would this teacher be lame?
Would this teacher be old
or like us, nowadays?

waiting, waiting

by Thara (Yr 6)

THE WORLD

The sun is hot,
but not a lot.
The sky is blue,
like something new.
The grass is green,
like something clean.
The trees stand tall
for all things small.
The sea is rough,
like something tough.
The moon is white,
like something bright.
The stars are fireworks
in the night.

by Palak (Yr 4)

TJ, TJ

TJ I miss you
TJ my love
Can't you come back to me,
snug as a glove?

TJ, TJ
Filled with power and might
quieter than the hush of a snowy night.

TJ, TJ
A hamster scared of loud bangs
TJ, TJ
Didn't we make a marvellous gang?

TJ I miss you
TJ my love
Can't you come back to me,
snug as a glove?

You may have died of a heart attack
But you're still alive in my heart.

by Maddie (Yr 5)

NURSERY

There I was, that girl with the cheeky smile
who runs around like a racing car
fascinating yummy treats like fruity lolly pops
and ice creams – happiness coming from all the screams.

The golden sun gives me a chirpy smile
inspired by its elegant bright grace
A special grin appearing from our soft smooth face.

"Come on girls and boys, there's some learning
that we all need to do about your shoelaces.
We love exploring from place to new places
and while we do it we need to be safe."

11:30, nearly 12… we're learning about numbers
and shapes, yay!
It's lunchtime now, I'll have a double sized
chocolate cake, Mmmmm!

Ooh look, here and there
exciting treats everywhere
even healthy things to eat
even fruits are a treat.

Oh look over there, a delicious green grape
like you can find anywhere, but not as special
like in here.

When the helpful teachers show me tricks for my art
I feel like a powerful dancer in the park.

I have the bestest friends with the goodest souls
They are the ones with the brightest hearts -
when I play with them, I am a nursery spark!

We learn about sharing and that helps me share -
This sentence, 'sharing is caring', that makes me stare.

I feel that I am a lucky girl
to be in this splendid colourful nursery world!

by Raisa (Yr 4)

MY HEAD'S WINTER WAR

I've got it, I really have,
the wind blows
dismal shadows upon us.
Over here, Miss, oh please,
downcast winter,
the frenzies,
thinking,
thinking.

Winter's come,
a terror out,
a heaven in.
I'm stuck, it's just too hard,
an ecstasy of bravery,
the beautiful relief,
the reigning belief,
the thumb war of life.

Twirl, twirl,
the twinkling spirit of the cold,
fading away forming,
forming,
winter's gone
a pile of snow,
the frenzies over,
the heart of cold,
Stella Stella
again and again,
I slept through class,
Believe it not
Thinking,
thinking.

The winter war,
my head's winter war…
Now for the History class.
Time passed by, Children
Blurred words begin to sink in

tick tock, tick tock
Time's up, school's over

My head's winter war.

by Daniella (Yr 6)

MY FUTURE

What will my future hold?
Will I be rich or will I be poor?
Will I do things bravely
or will nothing change about me?
Will my dreams come true
or will they not? Nobody knows
what my future holds.

Will I be a soldier
or will I be a clown?
I hope my life
doesn't turn upside down.
Will I have a good job or not?
Nobody knows
what my future holds.

by Taha (Yr 6)

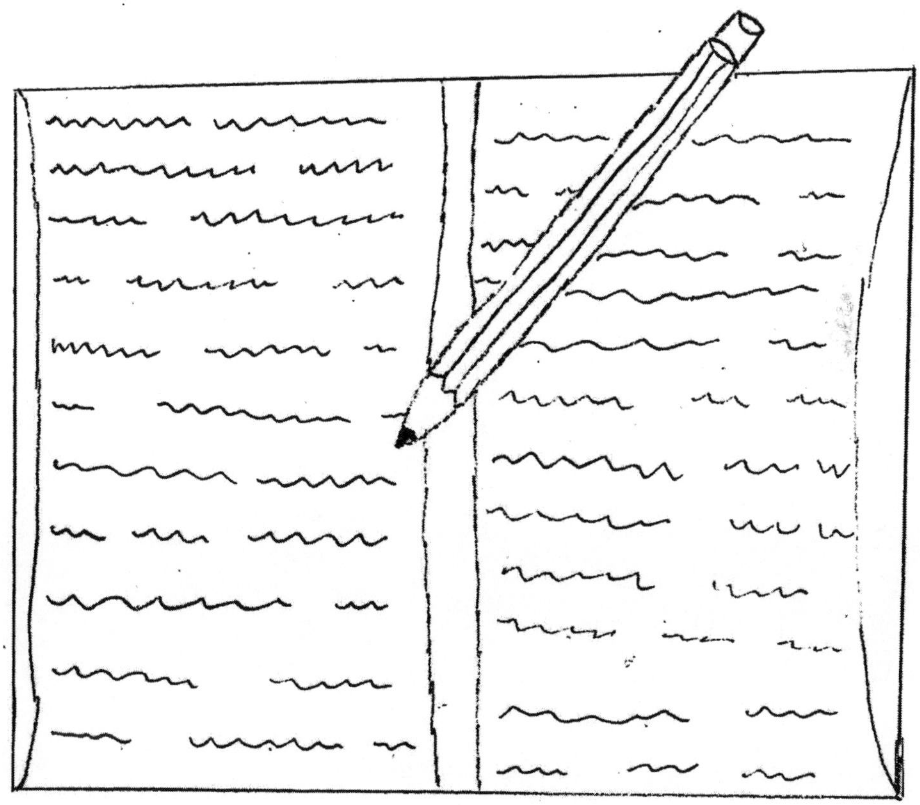

wild spaces

At Highfield we are lucky, our playground is full of nature and wild spaces to explore. We have animals, plants and even a pond where we can sit quietly and observe the world around us.

One sunny day I held Poetry Surgery by the pond and these are some of the poems that were written.

THIS POEM IS FOR EVERYONE

The waves slowly floating against the board
around the tiny tadpoles
under the water there is a shiny white rock.

The water is splashing
while the tadpoles are jumping
little fish swish their tails.

by Ayla and Anissa

THE POND

It's like a mirror in the wild
slowly swaying
lots of living creatures
like tadpoles and pond skaters
surrounded by plants and files
splishing and splashing
day and night.

by Yousra

THE BEES ARE BLACK AND YELLOW

The bees are black and yellow
and they sound like this – Buzz Buzz

The tadpoles in the pond
are swimming – Splish, Splash, Splosh

Rabbits, rabbits everywhere
they go like this – Sniff Sniff

Don't you just want to take them home?

by Lois

THE GREEN FROGS

Jumping upon us making strange noises
that no one can make
Little baby foxes looking in the see-through
mirror in front of them
Orange jelly ladybirds hopping onto
the baby's black nose

by Monika

AWOKEN

Tiny tadpoles glow
in the dark green water
foxes see their reflection
I can hear birds singing
the calm pond wakes me up

by Iman H

I CAN SEE

I can see the dark green sea
long grass, brown hard sticks
soft fluffy bushes wave slowly
there are pinecones and trees
hard rocks with flowers inside
the sea is like a mirror

by Zilan

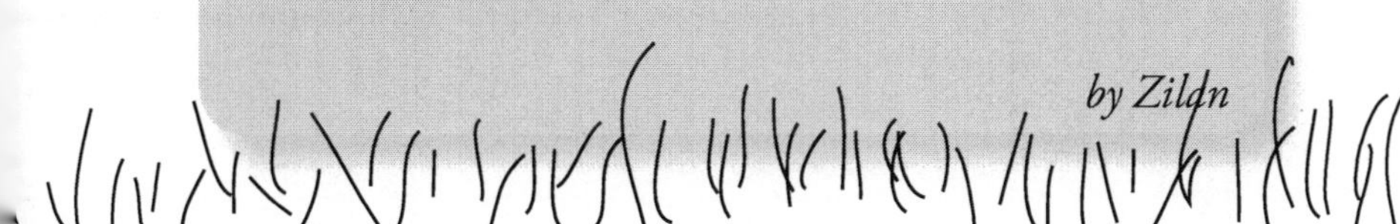

valuing values

A set of core values is at the centre of school life at Highfield, the primary amongst them being Respect, Co-operation and Kindness.

This year marks the eight hundredth anniversary of the signing of the Magna Carta and is an ideal opportunity to reflect on the crucial role it has played in the development of human rights, democracy and liberty.

At Highfield this year we have framed our thinking around:

FREEDOM and PERSEVERENCE

FREEDOM

After climbing a great hill
more and more
you can't be stopped

never
never

Free like a bird
Flapping
Flapping

never stop
never will

never
never

More hills
more excitement
stepping, stepping

Can't be stopped
never will

never
never

And after all one finds
that there are many more hills to climb.

by Jackson (Yr 5)

Holly (Yr 3), Ryan (Yr 4), Yekta (Yr 4), Alex (Yr 6), Maddie (Yr 5), Raisa (Yr 4), Joseph (Yr 5), Yousra (Yr 3), Thara (Yr 6), Sophia (Yr 6), and Jackson (Yr 5) are in the AMA group.

AMA stands for Amazing Minds Assemble.

Theirs <u>are</u> amazing minds and together we have done some amazing thinking and writing. Occasionally we try to weave all that thinking and writing together.

This is one of those attempts - AMA's Freedom Blanket Poem:

FREEDOM...!?

Captivity is a face without a smile, because a smile says it all!
Freedom is a smile because everyone has the right to be happy.

If you want to make peace with your enemy, you have to work with them
Then he becomes your partner.
My life is full of freedom when I am with my friends –
together we can achieve more!!!

Freedom is the pop and splash of a firework,
Freedom is a candle.

When I'm looking up at the sky, I see a butterfly so colourful and free.
My heart aches as it tries to be free,
to have a butterfly's freedom
Freedom is a butterfly!

Freedom is a flower blooming, because it is waking up to the yellow sun.
Purple flowers are free to grow anywhere.

Freedom is a field of purple flowers.
Captivity is a mask, because a mask covers who you really are.
Slavery is a man praying, because he is praying for his life.
Courage is not the absence of fear… but the triumph over it.
Freedom needs to be here, instead of locked behind bars over there.

No freedom is to be trapped in a chasm…
Open the gate to freedom!!!
Free to eat as much as you wish!

After climbing a great hill
more and more you can't be stopped.
Never, never… free like a bird
Flapping, flapping
never stop.

Freedom is a hot air balloon with a single person in it.
Freedom flies in colourful air when you are the only one there…
Finding the shapes of the clouds.

freedom writes

For most of the Winter and Summer term a group of six Year 4 children met during guided reading time to think about the theme of Freedom, and to write a book of verse to use with a Year 2 buddy group for guided reading.

Freedom Writes is: Mirela, Islimada, Callum, Heru, Jesse and Antonia. Later on the group was joined by Luke.

Here is some of the text from their book:

IMAGINE...

A bird in a cage, starving
An old horse being whipped
A dog trapped like a prisoner
A special tree being cut down in the jungle, the whole jungle dying

IMAGINE...

A baby crying, children with no one to look after them
A dog with no food or water
A pigeon left on the road with a broken wing
A flower cut because she is not beautiful

I am a flower, lying on the grass
They cut me down because they said
I was not as beautiful as the others.

Now see how empty the ground is
without me, and think how different
and sad the world would be without us.

We must all be free to be who we are.

A child at Highfield asked of me
Tell me, what does it mean to be free?

Let's find the answer together I said
I've written these words for you to read...

Freedom is a dog running happily in the park.

Freedom is magic in the sky.

Freedom is enchantment in your heart.

Freedom is wearing whatever you want.

Freedom is time to have fun with everyone.

Freedom is flying up in the air and reaching the clouds.

Freedom is time to travel, to explore the extraordinary world.

Freedom is reaching into your dreams and making it better.

Freedom is a rainbow that brightens the sky.

Freedom is standing outside at night, looking at the moonlight.

Freedom is the colour of nature, a bud blooming into flower

Freedom is the mighty elements in the air, and the windows onto nature.

Freedom is a lonely train, left in the jungle –
when you climb aboard you can go anywhere.

Freedom is a lonely pen that's never been used,
when you hold it in your hand, you could write anything.

Freedom is a door that leads to a magical world.

Freedom is a lost person, led by light.

A SHORT POEM ABOUT FREEDOM

Whether you are taking your dog to the park,
talking to your friends
watching a bird fly
skating out in the open
sitting under a warm blue sky
or eating fruit, just ripe...

Feel the flow
This is the happiness of freedom.

by Heru

Iman O's earthquake poem written after the terrible earthquakes in Nepal and other parts of the world, makes me think about perseverance – the difficulties and hardships that so many people have to face and the importance of never giving up on them.

EARTHQUAKE

Wind whooshing
and wishing in the world
People crying, lost their home
people lost, people that are poor
now why does it have to be them?
Why does it have to be anyone?
Why couldn't it be no one?
Just think how you would feel
if it was you – if it was a friend
you would help, these people
are human, you are one of the people
to help
please
help

by Iman O (Yr 3)

The pupils aren't the only ones using writing to contemplate values.

At a staff meeting I invited teachers to look through some old magazines and find images that might connect in some personal way with the idea of perseverance. Everyone's images were very different and produced some inspired pieces of individual writing which I have strung together here as:

POETRY ON PERSEVERENCE

wine, chocolate, high heels

Each drop
every splash
helps me
walk through
the gradient
ongoing
until
I pull through

French road sign, glass triangle at the Louvre, mosaic floor

When the avenue sign
affixed to the wall
looked down on all
the events that transpired below –
it pointed, informed, watched patiently.

Nebula of colours, space, eternity chaos, a tree in full blossom

In between
Space and Ground
Heaven and Earth
Beauty and Blossom
Are the bits and bobs
The Chaos of the life we live.

long road, large wave, cups balancing

The road is lonely
does not end
returning
again and again
engulfing
waiting to float
aimlessly on the calm sea

growth, time, resist

Problems, mistakes, solutions, ideas,
results flowering,
beautiful
Clocks ticking, continuous, endless
Tempting sweet… resist?
I can't.

knife, phone, teapot

Balancing on a knife edge
Tipping back and forth
Darkness looms below
But with a lifeline,
A shoulder, an ear, support
And an ocean of tea
I can do it.

bracelet, holiday, age smoothing cream

This bracelet is the never-ending circle
This holiday is the point of relaxation -
finally being in a better place.
And this pot of cream tells me
age has no limits.

chili, concrete towers, working out

Don't stop
It won't be easy
It will cause pain

We keep on going
to achieve a goal
to gain something
The point?

crosswords, brain, fitness

Wanting to get going, thinking it over,
then go!
I go slow, I ache, this is for me
this is my body.
For my mind
for my body
I will run.
I love to ache.
To think better, I will be positive
to look better, I will be me!

dancing in the rain. a flower surviving the storm, birds flying

Life is about
learning to dance
in the rain – no shame

Life is about surviving
the storm like a purple flower
alone but in bloom

Birds flying free
determined to reach
their destination, like me.

trapped razor, Canadian geese flying in formation, watch with different measure

Break free
don't watch
the clock
the time
hands ticking
fly past it
break out
of the ice block

desk, full cup, plant

Sitting at his desk
furrowing his brow;
His overflowing glass of lemonade
reminds him –
Keep going.
His plant says
"Grow".

old wooden clock, old couple in a frame, sofa/armchair

Time
9am. Days on repeat.
Light at the end.
Rest. Sofa.
It gets better.
Marriage. Life.
Years.

beyond

Reaching the moon, space, planets
coping on a long car journey
reaching a comfy sofa
at the end of the day
finally seeing
vibrant
blooming
flowers.

chocolate, time, car

A drive with the
window rolled down
allows my thoughts
to drift away
and the sun
shining through…
Need I say more?

16 words

I wait for time
to crawl
pass
turn rusty and old
A journey of a lifetime.

peaceful stranded island, family standing in the ocean, trainers

Staring out over the horizon,
children hand in hand
All we can hear are the sounds of the sea
and the song of the birds.
No phones beeping, game consoles
screeching, music playing.
Just the sound of happy hearts beating.
Busy lives
Peaceful for a time!

wine, birds flying, pack of wolves, mouth closed

Precious relaxation
time alone
Thoughts flying
free, roam
Don't say a
word
Let them bite…
ravenous!

washing up liquid, rocket, child with animals

Juggling
relationships, work, housework
Worth it in the end?
Final goal?

Building relationships
Inspiring lives
House proud – a home!
Happy!!

strength, belief, future (my dream)

Seek strength
don't look alone
seek belief
don't look alone
see your dream
dream alone.

by the teachers at Highfield

adventure a-z

Nearly time for the Easter break – look where Year 4 are going on their holidays:

THE A-Z OF PERFECT ADVENTURES

I am going to **A**rgentina on an **A**irplane and I am going to eat an **A**vocado

I will go to **B**razil on a **B**ig **B**rown **B**ear, I will go to a **B**each and make a big yellow sand castle

I can go to **C**anada to **C**ommune with **C**anaries

I am going to the **D**arling river on a **D**onkey to **D**ip my foot

I am going to **E**thiopia on an **E**normous **E**lephant and will be **E**ating an **E**gg.

I will go to **F**rance on a **F**ish and a **F**errari to explore the **F**rozen atmosphere

I will go to the **G**alapogas Islands on a **G**lider to gather **G**litter

I will go to **H**ighfield **H**ippo Farm on a **H**anging pig to be a **H**at maker, or to **H**ogar mountain on a **H**elicopter, looking quite **H**andsome

I will **I**ce-skate to **I**celand to eat **I**ce-cream and build an **I**gloo

I will travel to **J**apan on a **J**umbo **J**et to go to the **J**ungle and play with the animals

I am going to **K**enya on a **K**oala bear to become a **K**night!!

I want to go to **L**ebanon on a **L**eprechaun fighting a **L**ion!!

I will go to **M**exico with a **M**araca on a **M**otorbike

I will go to the **N**orth Pole to snow board and make a snow man, and do **N**othing but eat!!

I will go to **O**klahoma on an **O**strich eating **O**ysters

I will **P**addle to **P**anama with my **P**urple **P**oodle

I am going to the **Q**ueen's Palace on a **Q**uiet **Q**uest or I will stand in a **Q**ueue

I am going to travel to **R**ome by **R**acing car to **R**ace round the whole city

I am going to **S**icily to see my **S**ister and her **S**even **S**parrows

I am going to **T**ottenham to **T**ry to see some football

I am going to the **U**nited Kingdom on an **U**nderground train using my mum's **U**SB stick on her phone

I am going to the **V**atican City in a **V**an to visit the Pope!

I am going to the **W**hite sea on some **W**ishes to write my adventures

I will go to **X**i'an in an **X**-ray machine to go and play in the **X**ylophone concert

I am going to the **Y**ellow River to **Y**odel

I will go to the **Z**agros Mountains with a **Z**ebra and one day I will go to the **Z**oo

punctuality

Back to school for the summer term. What better way to start the new term than with an attendance campaign - a determination to be on time.

HIGHFIELD SCHOOL ATTENDANCE POEM

Some say it's cool
not going to school
Some think it's fine
never being on time

I've heard it said
that lying in bed
can be a good way
of spending the day.

Some say, why worry?
What's the big hurry?
Registration can wait
if you're a bit late.

I must suppose
such thinking arose
from those who don't know
how the rest of it goes....

The road is all quiet, there is no one about
They've gone from the door, Mrs Lynch, Mr. Blount
No welcoming face to wish me good morning
Just a voice in my head, whispering warning

The gate will be locked! Your classroom door closed!
You'll be marked in the book so everyone knows.

The school day has started without me again
I wish I was in there with all of my friends
There's a lump in my throat and my chest has gone cold
And the voice in my head has turned to a scold

You've missed quiet reading, and so much else too.
We all know what we're doing, all except you!

I'm tiptoeing in, they're all looking at me
I'm that person again, disturbing the peace
If I could, I would make this whole morning rewind
Tell the voice in my head to help me this time

Excellent attendance requires independence
plus assistance from home, so show them this poem –

Twenty-five to nine
You can do it this time
Imagine how cool
To be early to school

To get there before
They open the door
And be at your desk
Before all the rest

Imagine the huge smile
On the face of Mrs Kemal
Just think of the loving
you'll get from Ms McGovern!

Mr Wilson will cheer
Big grin, ear to ear
Ms Christadoulou
Will say hallejulah

Let's absent all the absences, reduce them to zero
Make all good attenders be Highfield school heroes!

Cheryl Moskowitz

I'M PUNCTUAL

I wake up so early
I'm happy as usual
I really love learning
I care about my future
I'm always prepared
I'm ready for school
I'm going to my classroom
I give homework too
I listen to my teacher
I want to be nice
I respect others
I am punctual!

by Martyna (Yr 2)

writing to art

In February the School council took a trip to the Wallace Collection. Here is a poem written by the School Council after that trip where they were helped by an artist to look closely at a painting by Rubens, *Landscape with Rainbow* (c.1636)

OUR TRIP TO THE WALLACE COLLECTION

First we took a train… we took one tube
and then another, till we got to the house.
The Wallace Collection.

The house was built 250 years ago
for the Duke of Manchester to be near duck shooting.
They wanted a house next to the river.

The last to have it, gave it to the public -
precious paintings, beautiful pictures,
lovely portraits. It was a precious house.

They wanted to leave everything out,
furniture, drawings, real paintings…
not put behind glass so it looked like a museum.

We saw the Laughing Cavalier
by a famous artist (but not in those days, only in these).

Rubens made a painting about the countryside.
a painting for himself, a landscape.
The painting was like a horizon,
dark at the bottom, light on the top.

Rubens used strong colours; purple, brown,
dark yellow and true blue. He mixed powder –
dust from rabbit bones -
with water, linseed oil and eggs.

Colourful pigment, blue dyes,
ultramarine, lapis lazuli from Afghanistan –
worth its weight in gold.
Pencil black graphite, earth red bole,
India yellow from cows' poo – cows
feeding on mango.

There were animals and workers in the painting,
a milkmaid in the foreground with cows, chickens and
ducks.

We looked at things in painting –
strong colours, shadow, light
three different kinds of green trees.

All things far away are light blue, pale blue
a blue picture of sky… and a rainbow.

by members of the School Council

The School Council took another trip in May to the National Portrait Gallery. This time they were helped by musicians from the English Touring Opera to look at a portrait and make a song about it.

A POEM ABOUT MAKING A SONG FROM A PICTURE

I raised my hand to Galaxy City
Curiosity rumbling inside me like a volcano
My body shaking like an earthquake
An excited shiver running up my spine
The painting we looked at was a whole different world
Wonder bubbles popped when the mystery was told
We made our own song
We made our own dance
We performed it in front of the picture
I was a caterpillar becoming a butterfly
I took a deep breath and emerged into the gallery
I was a shooting star
A star soaring off brightly into the dark sky
Pride and happiness fuming inside me
Bursting out of me like a rocket ship
Singing the song was like launching into space
I felt lucky and proud, standing tall as the Shard
I wanted to raise my hand in the air again and again
as if I had completed a 10 mile run.

What would I change? Very little, it's true
Only to stay longer, make our own portraits too.
The workshop enjoyable, educational, imaginative.
The gallery colossal, colourful and fun
The trip amazing (best ever!)
Thank you everyone!

by members of the School Council

the election

While the general election was taking place nationally, Highfield was busy organising its own hustings, campaigns and ballot boxes, as pupil candidates from each year group sought the support of their fellow pupil voters in their quest to become the new Pupil Head Teacher.

THE APPLICATION

First, are you our sort of person?
Are you... upbeat, optimistic,
someone who strives to see the bright side?
Do you have a way of spreading sunshine
even on the greyest day?

Would you describe yourself
as a person with drive, determination,
definite ideas and a burning desire to make them happen?
If there was a mountain, say, that needed climbing
would you make it to the top or stop half way?

How would you fare, do you think,
at sea, if your sails were set against
a railing wind and the full force of a mighty storm.
Would you hold steady, stay on course
or lose your nerve, abandon calm?

Can you judge and decide,
listen close to all sides. How are your ears?
Would you hear the quiet squeak of a mouse above the
loud roar of a lion? If someone was trying
to be understood, could you let them?

Finally, and perhaps
most importantly too. Does it fill
you with joy to be coming to school?
Is Highfield a place you can work in and play?
Would you like it to be your job every day?

Now, what do you think, do you fit
the description? Are you strong, fair and
passionate. Is smiling a feature? If so, persevere
and who knows, you could be, you might
very well be our new Pupil Head Teacher!

Cheryl Moskowitz

A SHORT HISTORY OF TIME

Time is a long rainbow, a quiet mouse, a hungry snake, a tall skyscraper...
We all know where it started –

A cave was made in the rainy forest
Mild winds made leaves shiver
as if they were surrounded by ice
and that's where it started to go wrong...

A deserted cave became an abandoned house
That lonely place became a building filled
with machines, computers created beyond our
imagination, taking risks previously unheard of

It is true what they say, machines changed time
Day by day these machines changed history
Who needs books said a person in the street
When you can have computers? (remember that house?)

The cave was abandoned, the house
demolished and turned into a school
The population of kids ignoring books
was ninety-nine percent... and me!

by George (Yr 6)

DON'T GET STUCK IN A WEB

There is a spider next to me making a web
while I am searching the web.
If I do something bad on the web
the spider might put me in its web.

Time can fly
but not for those flies in the spider's web.
The time of a fly in the web is like a snail getting to the finish line.

Still all I do is search the web
while the spider spins its own.
In the web are the flies who have done something bad.

They did what no one wanted to do
that is, to make the spider mad…

by Gleni (Yr 6)

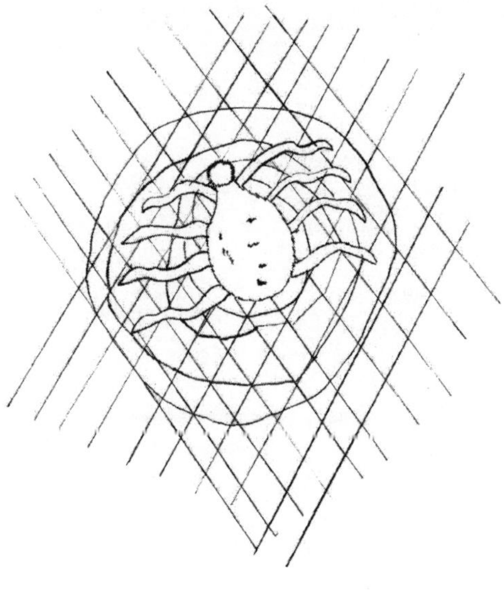

A TREE POEM

I.
A tree is sitting there, running out of time
I'm sitting here seeing how all of it works.
The fresh green grass, a person with an ice-cream cone
and I'm on my own
with no where to go
just watching the days go past.

I see a bird,
it spread the word across the world,
it may be the one.

Time is going past,
that tree is all I can remember,
hours are not worth waiting for,
it is going to be too late.

II.
A new computer has come out, new to here.
I had a little look inside and thought I saw
a tree outside, sitting there again.
New flowers blossoming
and the grass making its way up from the ground.
Someone might come and step on it
but the grass will never give up.

III.
I feel free on my own this day,
and then I saw that tree again,
thinking it was my granddad sitting there
when we used to have tea together and play, but maybe it's not.
And yes, the tree was going down slowly
its soul flowing away.
Trying to reach its arms out,
being strong.

I tried to make myself laugh,
a giggle, a little tickle…
but I couldn't help myself.
Let nature take its course,
let me find out for myself.

IV.
Back on the computer to see what will happen next.
I might end up on something else,
who knows?
Saving the tree
No Yes No Yes
Going through my head.

Sometimes you have to let things go, and this is one of them.

by Luisa (Yr 6)

WHAT I HEAR

A car is driving fast, I thought it was a flash
but it was just a dash of lovely colour
loads of different cars, big and small
the fresh green grass moves in the calm wind
I see a bird flying happily
I see the bird spreading the word…

I have been playing a game
only one minute left until
I reach the next level
if I can… 30 more seconds
I know I can do it
I won't give up
even though
I am running
out of time
5, 4, 3, 2, 1

Outside the colourful bird
is talking, playing and
talking, she spends almost
five hours a day with friends

I froze, time was up
I lost that round
I only did have
one more round
it may take months
years to get back
and I might lose
again

Oh dear
I need to
spend my time
on something else

Not just my computer

by Shima (Yr 6)

THE BUG WANTS TO KNOW

"What is time?"
The bug wants to know

I see the flowers blooming
Butterflies seem nice and sweet
but all they want
is the juicy information behind

"What is time?"
The bug wants to know

Mountains take ages to climb
But if I'm not quick enough
the mountain might
be swallowed by the sea

"What is time?"
The bug wants to know

Tick tock tick tock
Not even the old lady next door
remembers her childhood

"What is time?"
The bug wants to know

Running, running
my feet pound the crumbling ground
Everywhere I try to hide
the bug is already there

"What is time?"
The bug wants to know

by Jada (Yr 6)

THE TREE OF TIME

Don't let the computer eat all your time
Why can't that time be mine?
Us growing big and strong
Clocks ticking really fast

Trees getting taller
Us getting smaller
The tree of time is dying

Beautiful pictures, but what's behind?
Us getting older
But maybe not bolder

Will we see more of the world?

A zombie is being eaten up by time
Why can't this time be mine?
Time is going, going fast
It's now the end
The clock has stopped.

by Zoe (Yr 6)

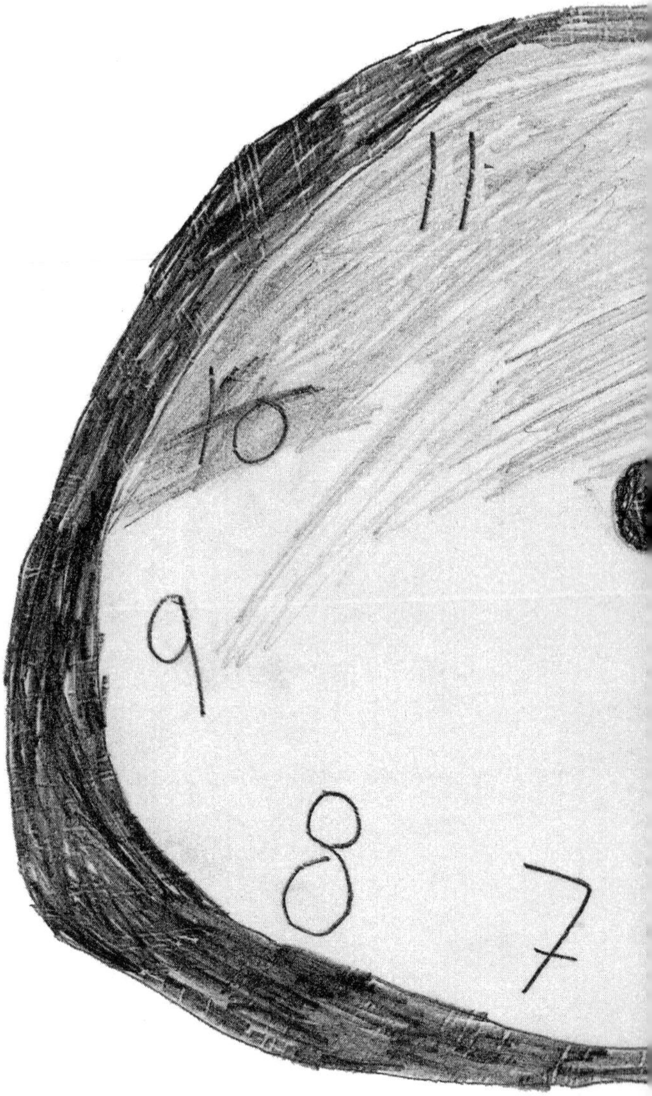

TICK TOCK

Minutes are passing like seconds
I don't think hours are going to last anymore
Days are dripping like water from a tap

A boy sits at his computer
Head bent in concentration
Will he ever reach the next level?

Months feel shorter than ever
Not enough time to do anything

Spring has come and the grass is starting to grow
bent over trying to reach the next level
will it ever reach the next level?

Trees are stretching their arms to the sun
but the storm is coming…
first a few drops, then a blizzard,
then lightning and then nothing
Just darkness because time is up…

by Sibel (Yr 6)

TIME IS LIFE

Time is an old photo
Time is a planted seed
Time is a butterfly come from a cocoon…

Time is life.

Time is a good thing, it will never go away
It is a great source that continues today.

Time made the Manta Ray, that has a sting
Time made the xylophone that has a loud Ping!

Even computers were made from time
Time is a computer's food.

A computer is an upgraded hoover
A computer contains forgotten information
Time goes on forever but a computer's battery will die sometime.

by Tyler (Yr 6)

Buxton Festival
Poetry Competition 2015
** COMMENDED POEM **

WILL IT BE?

How long does it take to squeeze out an orange?

Do you like porridge?

Will rockets ever fly to Jupiter?

Is there fog on Mars?

Will pigs ever fly? Will clothes ever dry?

Are famous people still going to be famous?

When people sneeze, can it make a shooting star fly across the sky?

Will Big Ben be the greatest clock? Will there be a 13 o'clock?

Will we go to the park? Is paper made from bark?

Will runners ever make it past the yellow mark?

Snails will go fast one day.

by Anastasia (Yr 6)

TICK TOCK TO FREEDOM AND ETERNITY

Cogs rotated inside
The hands moved to tell the time
Everyone thought it was ordinary
Tick Tock Tick Tock Tick Tock…

But when war struck like midnight
The tower clock was no more
Everyone was bewildered
Tick Tock Tick Tock…

Bombs cried through the sky
As the city turned to rubble
Still the war carried on
Tick Tock…

The minutes moved like hours
Hours crawled by like days
And the clock had its final cry
Ding Dong Ding Dong

It had nothing more to say.

by Alex (Yr 6)

MY MOTHER

If my mum was something I could put on, everyday
she would be a woolly jumper,
soft and snug.

If my mum was a sound,
she would be a cat's gentle purr
as I stroke its soft furry head.

If my mum was something I could eat
she would be a strawberry, mmmmmm....
my favourite treat.

If my mum was a feather
she could fly like a hot-air balloon
floating in the sky
like a butterfly in my heart.

by Yousra (Yr 3)

A SHORT POEM ABOUT MOTHERS

Mummy, Mum, mother
Thank you

by Alex (Yr 6)

WHEN GRANDPA...

On the winter holiday
I flew many hours on the plane
to visit my grandpa.
The stay was fun except this day
he was coughing and spluttering.
On one evening
he was wheezing loudly
for every gasp of air.
He couldn't sit up,
his eyes folded up
and his mouth opened
and he spoke gently, 'I love you'
and his hands dropped to the floor.
My dad shed tears
my mother tried to catch his soul
and I said in return
"Another 50 years and you'll see him in heaven."

by Alex (Yr 6)

TRUST AND BELIEVE

for Mum

On your drive home you can hear
the birds singing
and before you see
the decorated wood door
with a number 601
You have a picture of me
in your head
going to school happily
so you can relax.
At home you clean and cook
and listen to music on the tv
maybe you go to my Nan's house
to look after her
before you get me.
After school I wait
with my head down
When I see you I charge
in to your arms
and you ask me
what I did today
I tell you,
'I wrote this poem.'

by Korçan (Yr 4)

YOU DON'T NEED

You don't need money to have a good mum
or a room of diamonds

all you need is a good heart
and a mum to love!

by Ryan (Yr 4)

THE HIDDEN SECRET

I'm staring at the clouds
But all of this is true
Here comes the story of me
That's my family
Here comes me on a boat
There's a book with a flower
That's my diary
And there's me watching the clouds…
'Dinner time!!' Mum shouts loud
I'll go and have her lovely lasagna
and then I'll tell her everything
and point out the clouds.

by Yekta (Yr 4)

MY MOTHER

My mother, my mother
is like no other, she is so nice.
When I'm really thirsty,
she brings me lemonade with ice.

She cooks and cleans
she gives me peas,
and always reminds me
to say 'please'.

When I'm sad,
she'll lean in close
and say, 'There's nothing to feel sad about,
you know I love you most.'

by Sophia (Yr 6)

MY MUM IS...

My mum would help me if I felt down
My mum would make my lunch
My mum would sign a time out sheet
That's what my mum would do.

My mum would help me with my homework
My mum would tell me off
My mum would risk her life for me
That's what my mum would do.

My mum is different.

That's why I love her.

by Jackson (Yr 5)

POETRYZONE
I Love My Family
PRIZEWINNER

IT TAKES ME AWAY

I love my mum
I love her lots
But what's special
is her smell.
Her smell
takes me away
and if I could
I would take
her scarf
with me,
I would.
I would
put my face
in her scarf
and smell
her special smell
it takes me away.
Sometimes I smell
her when she kisses
me goodbye and
it takes me away.

by Holly (Yr 3)

MY LOVELY MUM

When I'm feeling sad or down, my lovely mum
asks me why, and I tell her. She then cheers me up.

When someone is rude to me, my lovely mum
tells me to ignore them, but if it keeps happening,
my lovely mum gives me lovely advice.

When I get home from school, my lovely mum
says, "How was your day?" If I say "Bad!" she listens
and cheers me up completely.

When I'm worried that I've failed at something
(but I never actually fail), my lovely mum tells me
it's alright and it's fine to make mistakes.

I love my lovely mum!

by Maddie (Yr 5)

MY MUM IS FOOD

100g of butter to soften her up
300g of sugar to sweeten her up
A pinch of chili to fire her up
50g of flour and mix her up
1tsp of essence to make her smell nice

3 pinches of brown sugar to tan her up right
2 tsp of baking powder to puffen her up right
A splash of love and a sprinkle of fun
Put her into the oven to get golden brown

A mother like mine is rare
so it would be right to call her 'mine'
with a four leaf clover to finish her off
to make her come alive,
that's why she is mine.

by Thara (Yr 6)

rainbow rhymes

At Highfield there are 58 different nationalities of children and 52 different languages spoken.

Rainbow Rhymes is made up of a group of children (and their parents) who speak many different languages but
are still in the process of learning English.

When we first met we told each other about what we loved and missed about our home countries, and thought about what we would most like to share with others who might not know what it is like to live there.

At Highfield Poetry has become a language everybody can speak, so we wrote this poem to tell everyone about us.

RAINBOW RHYMES—A POEM ABOUT US

I like Spain –
my family, my friends
the sea, the food, the animals, the city
I like the restaurants, I like what is new and old
The colour of my country is red on yellow, like a flower

Hola, adios, amigos,
bandera, vienen aqui
Hello, goodbye,
my flag, come here… I will show you.

In Bulgaria I like the sea, the animals, the flowers
At the centre of my city, I like the malls, shopping with my friends
I like the food in Bulgaria, I like the sun, the snow, the moon and the stars
I love my family and the colours of my country
white, green and red

Zdraveĭ, dovizhdane,
priyateli idvat tuk,
za snega

Hello, goodbye,
friends come here,
let me show you… the Bulgarian snow

I miss my friends and where I lived in Lithuania,
In my country, I love to play with my friends
When we are running they try to catch me
When it is snowing, we build a snowman

In Greece I miss my mother's pancakes
with cheese and ham inside
Souvlaki in pitta bread
with onions, tomatoes, chips
and Greek sauce that hides inside
My name means the juice of the gods

I miss the sun and the sea
With my friends every single day,
we would go with our bikes,
play games together.
Happy for me,
Always exciting.

In my country I feel so free.
With my family at the beach
swimming with the fish in the ocean.
Blue beaches, warm and wild
Black sea, wild and black

My name means 'Golden Mouth'
I love my Grandpa's chicken,
with its crispy skin and salad
My family is my Grandma and Grandpa
Black eyes, meat and pasta

Warm beaches with a shiny sparkle
Where the floor is like gold
covered with small crabs

Ela
Come!

I love my home in London
the view from the top of the hill
Ally Pally, the highest place in London
Good view, beautiful

My name means magic
I miss my mum because she is in Turkey
I miss the blue beach in Turkey
I miss my friends that I played with there
I like making snowmen, building snowmen
I miss going to my Turkey house,
I miss the Turkish school

I want to show you something special about where I'm from…
Come with me.

RAINBOW RHYMES looked at a poem called 'Considering the Snail' by an American poet called Thom Gunn – we liked the ideas and images in the poem so Rainbow Rhymes made up their own version.

You can find Thom Gunn's original poem by searching on the internet. We think it is a beautiful poem with an important message about perseverance and not giving up.

RAINBOW RHYMES CONSIDERS THE SNAIL

after Thom Gunn

A snail is looking for his way
in a dark night when it rains and thunders
The night is usually blue
but tonight the moon is bright
and the grass is wet
It is a green night
The snail crosses the green wet grass
Slithers so slowly, looking round and round
His purpose is to learn about life in another world.
He has found lots of animals in the forest
but can't say to them to help him
The snail's antlers are bright
but they don't have a lot of power
See how lightly he makes his way
where water drops have darkened the ground
The snail is not too strong
but he never gives up
In a dark rainy night
he walks in a wood of power
I didn't know anything about a snail's fury
How to try and never give up
So slow, but pushing himself
quicker and quicker
the snail is small
but can
survive.

At Highfield poetry has become a central part of the school's life. Not all schools have a resident poet and not all people necessarily even know what a poem is or what it might be good for. School Council decided to write a poem to let people know.

poetry at Highfield

WHAT IS A POEM?

a poem is a lie that tells the truth
a poem is a bright light in the darkness
a poem is a dazzling library of stories
a poem is a sword, sharp and sly
a poem removes the blindfold so that we can see the world more clearly
a poem is your heart, counting the minutes to your death
a poem is a single star in the night sky
making a poem is like having three wishes
a poem is a clever monkey maneuvering round the jungle to reach the best fruit on the highest tree
a poem is a rainbow leading to treasure
a poem is a lost treasure drowned in tears
a poem is a never-ending story, a magical myth you can believe in
a poem is a fire-breathing dragon, a fierce strong bear
a poem is a sweet melody that brings harmony
a poem is soft as feathers and sweet as a baby lion
a poem is a memory
a poem is remembering
a poem is being remembered
and never forgotten.

WHAT CAN A POEM DO?

a poem can blow you away
a poem can touch your heart
a poem can put a smile on someone's face
a poem can be an embrace
a poem can shine a light on people's stories
a poem can change people's minds
a poem can be a doorway to history
a poem can be a doorway to freedom
a poem teaches us about rules
a poem lets you make your own rules
a poem makes you the ruler of your room, your mind, your pen
a poem makes use of our ideas, puts our values into action
a poem can inspire us to read more and to write more
a poem can help us understand the past in new ways
a poem helps us know the world and our place in it
a poem helps us know what's most important
a poem tells others who we are, what we know, what we want and what we believe…
a poem can change your life!!!

SINCE HAVING POET IN OUR SCHOOL...

we are thinking more creatively about what we want now and in the future
we are learning more about ourselves and other people
we are using poetry to put ourselves in other people's shoes and communicate important messages like anti-bullying.
we are using poetry to communicate our beliefs, thoughts and feelings to the wider world.
we are sharing memories through poetry and bringing poetry into the community
we are spreading important messages about core values like friendship, respect, close cooperation and freedom.
we are writing about important subjects like war and peace – our poems are winning prizes, published and displayed in key public places like the Wiener Library for the study of Holocaust and Genocide.
we are changing people's minds about children
we are raising our standards and achieving more!
we have become more confident in our reading and writing
we have become more imaginative in our thinking
we are feeling inspired
we have increased our vocabulary
we have improved our listening and speaking skills
we are entering competitions
we are making the headlines (local and national newspapers are writing about us and the poetry we are making)
we are bringing pride and fame to ourselves and our school.

WHAT IS SO SPECIAL ABOUT HAVING A REAL LIVE POET IN OUR SCHOOL?

Our school poet is a professional poet. She brings her experience and a special kind of knowledge and understanding about how to write poems and shows us how poetry can be important in all of our lives.

She is someone we can go to when we have an idea and she helps us turn our ideas into poems that can be shared.

Having a poet in the school has made Highfield (which is already the best school in the world) even better!!

year 6 road poems

The Road Not Taken
by Robert Frost (1917)

Two roads diverged in a yellow wood,
And sorry I could not travel both
And be one traveler, long I stood
And looked down one as far as I could
To where it bent in the undergrowth;

Then took the other, as just as fair,
And having perhaps the better claim,
Because it was grassy and wanted wear;
Though as for that the passing there
Had worn them really about the same,

And both that morning equally lay
In leaves no step had trodden black.
Oh, I kept the first for another day!
Yet knowing how way leads on to way,
I doubted if I should ever come back.

I shall be telling this with a sigh
Somewhere ages and ages hence:
Two roads diverged in a wood, and I—
I took the one less traveled by,
And that has made all the difference.

As their time at Highfield nears an end, Year 6 looked back on their primary school journeys, from Nursery through to the end of Year 6. They also considered what new roads may lie ahead as they move on to Secondary School.

Year 6 pupils took inspiration from this famous poem by American poet Robert Frost (1874 – 1963).

Inspirational poems like Robert Frost's are often quoted.

Year 6 wrote such beautiful 'road' poems of their own that I thought their work should be quoted from too.

Here is a selection of extracts, three short lines from each:

No limit to where I can go.
The frost-white moon cackles,
time slows down but I will not give up.

Saaqib

Gazing at the white light above her,
she only wished
to conquer her fears.

Aiya

Sitting silently on the brown branch,
watching the free birds
glide in the cobalt sky.

Ferdows

Imagine this: one traveller, two roads,
shadows gradually appearing.
Remembering the past.

Luka

The sound of the wind
whispering in my ear.
The clouds covered the sun.

Braw

Ancient trees like bodyguards,
a green blanket across smooth hills.
He leapt like a frog over the gap, laughing all the way.

Nadeer

Two roads; one dull and faded,
the other bright and fresh.
A smile on the path.

Hadiza

I dance, I laugh,
a glow of determination.
Bright drops of gold wrinkled over the blue.

Hanan

Learn to make rain your friend,
wash away the grit and stone.
Be guided by the wind.

Stephen

Higher and higher,
I thought there would be no end
until I saw the sun.

Angelos

Soaring towards the target,
crossing the impenetrable,
step by step believing, I've done it.

Victor

Bright as a cluster of stars, the sky.
The sun, a bright yellow bulb.
I leap from rock to rock.

Stephan

I want to have
a lot of friends.
I will be happy for that

Vinamin

Waiting for the storm to pass,
waiting for the sun to rise.
Rain on my face, let it be. A rainbow rises ahead.

Nickolas

Two roads part from the main path.
Slow and steady, wins the race;
I keep on walking.

Sammie

Trepidatious, she balances on a branch
and begins climbing
the never ending ladder.

Yasha

Leisurely autumn comes and runs.
Trees die and ice mountains replace flowers.
Her heart is the sound of drums and an eagle passing by.

Thara

School is so big,
my friends are kind and funny,
my heart beats like a drum.

Elena

Here for the first time,
I thought it was going be difficult
but I made friends and it was easy.

Nicolas

An uncertain journey,
I step through
an enchanted door.

Dever

A new chapter.
Empty spaces are waiting
for me to fill.

Misbah

The ocean is pushing me further, to my new adventure.
Something new is waiting for me.
Before I go in I'm going to breathe the fresh air.

Chris

I'm heading to a new world.
Everything is unknown,
soon everything will be shown.

Tyler

Dark clouds hover,
broken bridge like a broken heart.
I look across the empty plain to see my world.

Nina

My life is like a long path
following me everywhere,
a beautiful line of story.

Zyle

I dance upon the yellow road,
I dance in the bright green grass,
I hide in the misty shadow, a new world to look for.

Pirlanta

It all began when the apple fell.
I opened the door to a new beginning,
the hills smiled at me and I smiled back.

Anastasia

In some chapters you need
to jump over a gate to see the future -
the pin drops and everything is stopped in time.

Zuzanna

What's next? says the boy in the street.
Only the future knows, I said.
Should I go or should I stay?

George

The bright sun shining light over me,
I dance under it
and feel free.

Taha

There is no choice but the other path.
Something's there, hiding behind the trees.
Happiness reveals itself to me

Daniella

A bridge is my path to the next chapter,
trees lure me into the unknown.
Nobody can stop me.

Tammy

Grey clouds swirling,
I danced in the rain.
Shadows start to fade away.

Atakan

Almost gold,
a crossroad.
Which way do I go?

Rebar

A traveller
looking back from my life,
Steadily climbing.

Jamari

I felt a little push,
not the kind that knocks you down,
but the kind that encourages you to try harder.

Nino

The breeze pushed me on
gently calling,
climbing the steep hill.

Alina

A new path,
no twists, no turns,
nothing but footprints.

Ameera

The success of my skills,
encouraging me to go forward.
I learned to dance in that rain.

Kadri

Looking back beyond the worn down bridge,
my teacher always there.
I see fog clearing, trees and flowers grow.

Abbey

Dark clouds come together
but never making darkness.
The hills in front are smiling.

Dumitru

An echo: so far yet so close,
the sweet smell of honey
fills the air.

Sophia

The path, not always smooth
has been worn well,
for now I stand on the bridge.

Mahsheed

Open fields with dancing butterflies,
the sun is an orange balloon
that constantly heats the world.

Isobella

Gazing back, it has gone so fast.
The sun was out like a shining star,
my success was a good one.

Ja'lan

White clouds engulf the road,
rain washes the stony path
and the darkness away.

Hope

Apples, oranges and grapes grew
ripe and sweet
where I learnt to dance.

Miki

A never fading rainbow arises.
A pot of gold
shining.

Ranim

THE LESSON

Summer wriggles closer
and each lengthening day
is a picture, another one
for the album.
In every child's face
a new poem smiles
its beginning.

The end of term
is the start
of something… special.

School teaches us this.

Cheryl Moskowitz

AUTHOR'S ACKNOWLEDGEMENTS

Thanks to all the pupils at Highfield for their wonderful poetry.

Thanks to the following children for their book illustrations in this book:
Adrien, Ameera , Antonia, Daniella, Ellie, Emilia, Emily, Fiona, Franky, Isabella, Joe, Kaan, Kristian, Leart, Linda, Mirela, Nadia, Nusrat, Oliver, Ollie, Parisa, Rema, Saphira, Selina, Tobias, Vash, Zahra, Zilan, and Zuzanna.

Thanks to all the teachers, staff and parents at Highfield for their support, enthusiasm and participation this past year.

Special thanks to Ms Wren for co-running the AMA group, to Mr Wilson and Mr Blount for sharing their time and office space so generously, to Ms McGovern for her constant support and for dreaming up the idea of having a resident poet in the first place, and finally to Mrs Kemal for her passion and determination to make it all possible.

Thanks and huge gratitude to Alastair Gavin for his tireless work designing this book.

Organisations/poetry competitions referred to in this anthology:
Wiener Library **www.wienerlibrary.co.uk**
ReWrite **www.rewrite.org.uk**
Poetry Zone **www.poetryzone.co.uk**
Buxton Poetry Competition **www.buxtonfestival.co.uk**

HIGHFIELD PRIMARY is a three form entry school in North London. When you visit you will instantly notice happy children, full of energy and enthusiasm. Highfield is an inclusive school where linguistic and cultural diversity is valued. Each child is encouraged to excel and have the skills, independence and initiative to become good citizens.

www.highfieldprimary.co.uk

CHERYL MOSKOWITZ is a poet and writing facilitator, who regularly visits schools. Previously an actor and playwright, she is trained in dramatherapy and psychodynamic counselling, and is a member of NAWE (National Association of Writers in Education). She co-founded LAPIDUS, the organisation for writing for well-being, and has taught for the Poetry School and on the Creative Writing & Personal Development MA at Sussex University from its inception in 1996. Her poetry has won several awards and her work features widely in literary magazines and anthologies. Her publications include the novel *Wyoming Trail* (Granta 1998), poetry collection *The Girl Is Smiling* (Circle Time Press 2012), and a book of poetry for children, *Can It Be About Me?* (Frances Lincoln Books 2012). She lives in North London.

www.cherylmoskowitz.com